"Honoring the Past; Creating the Future"

This Member Manual Belongs to:

Name	
Date Started Training	
Instructor's Name	
Federation ID	

Gain a deeper understanding of the Founder's lifetime achievements through these publications:
"History of The Moo Duk Kwan®" and the *"Moo Do Chul Hak"*

DEDICATION

This Member Manual is dedicated to the Founder Hwang Kee and the rich history of his Moo Duk Kwan® organization and the Soo Bahk Do® martial art system he created.

His personal actions as demonstrated throughout his life have become the Moo Do theory embraced by thousands of Moo Duk Kwan® members worldwide and employed in the practice of the Soo Bahk Do® martial art.

A special thank you to Founder Hwang Kee and the continued leadership of H.C. Hwang Kwan Jang Nim. Each of us as practitioners now have the powerful and personal opportunity to improve the quality of our life and the quality of the lives of those around us by embodying and demonstrating Moo Do Values in all our actions.

Copyright 2019

United States Soo Bahk Do Moo Duk Kwan Federation®

Contents may not be duplicated without written permission.

Federally protected Trademarks and Service marks

United States Soo Bahk Do Moo Duk Kwan Federation®

United States Tang Soo Do Moo Duk Kwan Federation®

Soo Bahk Do®

Moo Duk Kwan®

The fist logo

The Official Soo Bahk Do Logo

Moo Duk Kwan® and the fist logo are federally registered trademarks of the United States Soo Bahk Do Moo Duk Kwan Federation®. Soo Bahk Do® and the Soo Bahk Do logo are service marks of the United States Soo Bahk Do Moo Duk Kwan Federation® and may not be used without written permission.

TABLE OF CONTENTS

GREETING FROM THE KWAN JANG NIM 6
WELCOME! 8
A BRIEF HISTORY OF SOO BAHK DO AND THE USA FEDERATION 10
WHAT IS THE UNITED STATES SOO BAHK DO MOO DUK KWAN FEDERATION? 12
WHAT IS THE UNITED STATES SOO BAHK DO MOO DUK KWAN FOUNDATION? 14
YOUR FEDERATION'S STRUCTURE 15
FEDERATION OFFICIALS 16
CONTACTING FEDERATION HEADQUARTERS & OFFICIALS 17
MISSION 2000 19
BENEFITS OF FEDERATION MEMBERSHIP 20
MEMBERSHIP CODE OF CONDUCT 25
REGIONAL STRUCTURE 26
OPPORTUNITIES OF FEDERATION MEMBERSHIP 27
AUTHENTIC LEGITIMATE RANK CERTIFICATION 28
DO JANG OWNERSHIP OPPORTUNITIES 29
INTERNATIONAL GOODWILL OPPORTUNITIES 30
YOUTH LEADERSHIP PROGRAM 31
VISION OBJECTIVES: "A LIVING ART; LIVING THE ART" 33
YOUR PERSONAL TRAINING EXPERIENCE 35
THE FIVE MOO DO VALUES 38
THE EIGHT KEY CONCEPTS 46
TEN ARTICLES OF FAITH ON MENTAL TRAINING 48
5 REQUIREMENTS & 11 POINTS OF EMPHASIS ON MENTAL TRAINING 49
5 REQUIREMENTS & 10 POINTS OF EMPHASIS ON PHYSICAL TRAINING 49
GUIDELINES FOR TRAINING 50
UNIFORM & BELTS 51
THE FLAGS 53
COURTESY AND ETIQUETTE 55
KOREAN TERMINOLOGY 59
    COURTESY AND ETIQUETTE 59
    GENERAL TERMINOLOGY 59
    COMMANDS IN TRAINING 61
    COMMANDS IN STARTING AND ENDING CLASS 61
    NUMBERS (BON) 62
    BASIC STANCES (GI CHO JASEH) 62
    HAND TECHNIQUES (SOO GI) 63
    FOOT TECHNIQUES (JOK GI) 65
    SPARRING (DAE RYUN) 66
    ANATOMY 66
    TOURNAMENT TERMINOLOGY 67

Soo Bahk Do® Moo Duk Kwan® Rank Progression Overview 68
Tiger Tots Achievement & Belt Ranking System 70
Soo Bahk Do® Moo Duk Kwan® Technical Curriculum 72
   9th Gup 73
   8th Gup 75
   7th Gup 76
   6th Gup 78
   5th Gup 80
   4th Gup 82
   3rd Gup 85
   2nd Gup 87
   1st Gup 89
   Cho Dan 91
   E Dan 92
   Sam Dan 94
   Sa Dan 96
   O Dan 98
   Yuk Dan 100
   Chil Dan 103
The Moo Duk Kwan Dan Bon 104
The Soo Bahk Do Moo Duk Kwan Ko Dan Ja Shim Sa 108
   Overview of the Ko Dan Ja Shim Sa Process 109
Instructor Certification Overview 110
   Jo Kyo Certification 114
   Kyo Sa Certification 115
   Kyo Bom Certification 116
   Sa Bom Certification 117
Rank Promotion Process 118
Obtaining School Certification 121
Transfers from Outside the Federation 123
Competition Overview & Tournament Rules 124

H.C. Hwang, Kwan Jang Nim

Serving as the President of the World Moo Duk Kwan and Life President of United States Soo Bahk Do Moo Duk Kwan Federation®

Greetings! Congratulations on becoming a member of the United States Soo Bahk Do Moo Duk Kwan Federation®, the home of the Moo Duk Kwan® in the United States of America.

Our art is deeply connected with the values of History, Tradition, Philosophy, Discipline & Respect, and Technique, which we call "The 5 Moo Do Values." We have been promoting these values since the Moo Duk Kwan was created by our founder in 1945 and thereafter, many practitioners like yourself worldwide have diligently preserved our art by adding their contributions to its rich history. We are glad to have you add your energy toward its continuing progress.

You will have many opportunities to better understand, embody and help strengthen the 5 Moo Do values in your classes and in Federation events that will provide regional, national, and international connection opportunities with fellow members. From these experiences, your identity as a Moo Duk Kwan member and Soo Bahk Do practitioner will grow and your Moo Do example will naturally and positively impact those around you in your community. As a result of your personal actions, we envision these values becoming more visible in communities, nations, and worldwide. I am looking forward to your active participation and support for the "Vision in Action."

We are proud to know that you will be taught by the Federation's best trained and educated Kyo Sa, Kyo Bom and Sa Bom who will guide your study during your Moo Do journey.

This member manual is prepared for all levels including Gup, Dan, Ko Dan Ja, Instructors, future instructors, school owners, future school owners and Federation Officials. I trust you will find useful and educational information and resources in it that will help support you in all your endeavors.

I extend my best wishes to you for a long and rewarding membership in the Federation that will provide you with unlimited opportunities and Moo Do experiences.

May God bless you, your work and your loved ones.

In Moo Duk Kwan,

H.C. Hwang

H.C. Hwang Kwan Jang Nim:
Brief Biography & Accomplishments

- Born March 4, 1947
- 1954, May 5: Entered the Moo Duk Kwan discipline
- 1957, October 27: Promoted to Cho Dan (1st Dan) in Moo Duk Kwan
- 1959, March: Graduated Yong San Elementary School
- 1962, March: Graduated Sun Rin Middle School
- 1965, March: Graduated Yang Jong High School
- 1965, November 15: Promoted to Sa Dan (4th Dan) in Moo Duk Kwan
- 1969, September: Graduated Korea University (Major in Philosophy)
- 1970, May 24: Promoted to O Dan (5th Dan) and Sa Bom in Moo Duk Kwan
- 1970-1973: Served as the Chief Sa Bom at the Central Headquarters Do Jang
- 1973-1974: Served as the Chief Moo Duk Kwan Sa Bom in Athens, Greece
- 1975, June 30 – 2002, July: Served as the Chairman of Technical Advisory Committee of the U.S. Tang Soo Do Moo Duk Kwan Federation
- 1978, January: Featured on cover of Black Belt Magazine
- 1980, March: Featured on cover of Black Belt Magazine
- 1984, September: Featured on cover of Black Belt Magazine
- 1989 – 2002, July: Served as the Vice President for the World Moo Duk Kwan
- 1999, August 31: Promoted to Gu Dan (9th Dan) in the Moo Duk Kwan.
- 2002, July - Present: Serving as the President of the World Moo Duk Kwan and Life President of U.S. Soo Bahk Do Moo Duk Kwan Federation.
- 2005, July: Inducted into the Black Belt Hall of Fame as "Man of the Year" (featured on the cover – Black Belt Magazine).
- Learn more: https://moodukkwanhistory.com/h-c-hwang/

Welcome!

Your fellow Federation members welcome you as one of our newest members!

Your Certified Instructor and Certified Do Jang Owner has

introduced you to the home of a warm and caring family of martial artists who are members of communities comprising the United States Soo Bahk Do Moo Duk Kwan Federation®. You now share a common bond and a common cause with all members of our 501c4 non-profit members' organization chartered to pursue the promotion of, public recognition of, and study of the Soo Bahk Do® martial art system as taught by Moo Duk Kwan® Founder Hwang Kee. You are now officially recognized as a "member in good standing" in one of the most prestigious and long standing martial art organizations in the world.

Your Instructor is a Federation member who has chosen to elevate their study and practice of Soo Bahk Do® to make a significant difference in the world by helping others like yourself to learn Soo Bahk Do® and the Moo Duk Kwan organization's history, traditions, philosophy, discipline/respect and techniques that can enhance practitioner's lives and by example and personal action, positively influence society.

Your Do Jang owner is a Federation member who has chosen to make a significant difference in the world by actively advocating Soo Bahk Do® training to the general public and by seeking to share our art's Moo Do values with even more students like you.

Your exciting new journey into the world of Soo Bahk Do® is made possible today by the convergence of your instructor's personal commitment to the Moo Duk Kwan® philosophy and through their membership in the Federation that has supported them along their path in order for them to be able to serve you today.

As you read through your membership manual you will learn much more about the living art that you are studying and the rewarding experiences and opportunities that await you as a Federation member.

You will also learn about the:

- Benefits that training will bring into your life.
- Opportunities you will have to pursue rank certification and even someday potentially making a significant difference in the world by becoming a certified instructor and /or Do Jang owner.
- Federation's history, its founders, its structure, its officials, and how your membership dues support your Federation to pursue its Chartered Purposes, Mission 2000, and the President's Vision Objectives.

You will also learn how to connect with fellow members across the nation, international affiliates around the world, and how you can become a leader in your Do Jang and your local community.

Many rewarding and exciting opportunities and experiences await you as a Federation member connected to a network of martial artists that spans the nation and the globe.

You can join some of the most active members in your new global network at your Federation's web site (https://soobahkdo.com/).

During your study, your Certified Instructor will assure your rank accomplishments are properly documented and legitimately certified by Moo Duk Kwan® president, H. C. Hwang Kwan Jang Nim and recorded on your permanent member record to document your history as a legitimate Moo Duk Kwan® member and Soo Bahk Do® practitioner.

You can be proud of the legitimacy and credibility of your accomplishments because the United States Soo Bahk Do Moo Duk Kwan Federation® is the only organization in the United States authorized to issue Moo Duk Kwan® rank certification in the martial art of Soo Bahk Do®. Once again, congratulations and welcome to the home of the Federation's family of Moo Duk Kwan® practitioners. "The Federation" is "every member" and we are happy you've joined us as a member-owner of the United States Soo Bahk Do Moo Duk Kwan Federation®.

Welcome to your Federation!

A Brief History of Soo Bahk Do® and the Federation

https://soobahkdo.com/history/

Soo Bahk Do® is Hwang Kee's unique interpretation of a Korean traditional martial art whose history dates back many centuries. Kicking techniques, for which Soo Bahk Do® is renowned, are an integral part of the Moo Duk Kwan® school's curriculum developed by the late founder Hwang Kee. Soo Bahk Do® is both a hard and soft style.

Founder Hwang Kee was a martial arts prodigy, having mastered Tae Kyun (another Korean system not related to Tae Kwon Do) at the age of 22. At that time (1936), he traveled to Northern China where he encountered a Chinese variation of martial artistry. From 1936 to 1945, he combined Eastern wisdom and developed what is now known as Soo Bahk Do®.

Soo Bahk Do is not a sport. Though it is not essentially competitive, it has great combat applications. As a classical martial art, its purpose is to develop every aspect of the self, in order to create a mature person who totally integrates his/her intellect, body, emotions, and spirit. This integration helps to create a person who is free from inner conflict and who can deal with the outside world in a mature, intelligent, forthright, and virtuous manner.

To promote and preserve the aforementioned qualities of his Soo Bahk Do® martial art system, Founder Hwang Kee named his first school the 'Moo Duk Kwan' and over time his schools have become a global force that is one of the most influential martial art organizations in modern times.

Moo Duk Kwan® certified instructors teach practitioners to strive to be a "brotherhood and school of stopping inner and outer conflict and develop virtue through Soo Bahk Do training."

- The unique Moo Duk Kwan® name gives us identity, direction and focus in our mental training. Soo Bahk Do® is the technique; the Moo Duk Kwan® organization guides the philosophy.
- Soo Bahk Do® technique requires the mental discipline that Moo Duk Kwan® schools compel.

The two combined produce a total development that increases the benefits of both. From their harmony is created an awareness of being that makes Soo Bahk Do® training a valuable art form as taught in Moo Duk Kwan® schools.

Since 1945, thousands of Americans have studied Soo Bahk Do® in Korea. Hwang Kee sent Korean instructors around the world and there are now major Moo Duk Kwan® organizations worldwide. As of 2019 there are roughly 200,000 registered Soo Bahk Do® practitioners and over 50,000 are Dan rank holders. Those who studied with the Grandmaster relate how demanding he was. (He was once heard to say: "If you want to do front and reverse punches correctly, you must spend ten hours a day, six days a week for three years doing nothing else.")

Prior to 1974 there were many Americans holding degrees and teaching and promoting without standardization, regulation, communication, or leadership. The Grandmaster decided that a United States organization must be established to unify and standardize the art.

As a result of this decision, the United States Soo Bahk Do Moo Duk Kwan Federation® was formed in 1975, guided by an elected and appointed Board of Directors, and originally operated by volunteer members. Chartered as a 501(c)(4) non-profit organization, the Federation is devoted to the growth and long-term preservation of the Moo Duk Kwan® organization and the Soo Bahk Do® martial art system in the United States and to maintaining the standards of excellence established by Founder Hwang Kee.

It is of testament to the Founder and his teachings that he commanded such respect and devoted effort from so many mature, intelligent, independent individuals, and the Charter Members who worked to create the Federation and those who were elected to the Board of Directors. There are certain qualities that characterize the Founder, the members of the Board, and Soo Bahk Do® practitioners in general— openness, personal closeness, independence, rock-hard determination, maturity, and unshakable solidarity. These qualities bind us together as kinsmen. This, more than anything else, assures future generations will have the opportunity to embrace the unique Moo Duk Kwan® curriculum during their study of the Soo Bahk Do® martial art.

U.S Federation Concept of Unity

"The Federation's purpose is to prepare a home in the United States for a unified Moo Duk Kwan assembly. It must earn the right and the privilege of having many Master, Dan, and Gup members who study Soo Bahk Do.

As a vehicle that promulgates the Korean Martial Art of Soo Bahk Do, it must keep developing the environment, atmosphere and respectability that will encourage many individuals to join in this unification effort and process.

The home that is being built must be a warm, comfortable and peaceful place that can be respected by all the Moo Duk Kwan stylists. It should have the ability to understand and serve each member's needs.

The present Federation members are the carpenters of this home. If the job is well done, tenants will surely move in and the Moo Duk Kwan assembly will finally have a home in the United States other than in their minds and hearts."

WHAT IS THE UNITEDSTATES SOO BAHK DO MOO DUK KWAN FEDERATION®?

First, last, and always, your Federation is a members' organization focused on teaching and promulgating the Moo Do values of Moo Duk Kwan® organization and preserving the Soo Bahk Do® martial art system as intended by Founder Hwang Kee.

The word "Federation" means a group of individuals bound together by a common cause and the Federation's 501c(4) non-profit status conveys that our cause is for the general good of the community. The Federation is neither a company nor a governmental body. It is every member working toward a common objective.

Your Federation is not a building, a person, or an employee; it is "every member." It is every instructor and every student. When we say, "the Federation," we are referencing ourselves because "every member" is the Federation. Because of that fact, the good things about the Federation are credited to every member, past, present, and future.

Your Federation's primary purpose is promoting the study of our martial art and working toward world peace by improving human relationships through the study of our art. We look forward to your personal contributions toward these goals and want to ensure that you enjoy the most rewarding experience possible as a member.

WHY IS THE U.S. FEDERATION NON-PROFIT?

Our Federation exists to assure the long-term preservation of the Moo Duk Kwan® organization and the Soo Bahk Do® martial art by serving and helping every practitioner excel and achieve the highest possible level of personal growth and success through their study and practice of Soo Bahk Do®.

The Federation operates as a non-profit entity to assure the maximum amount of member resources are re-invested in supporting member opportunities to grow, excel and prosper. Through your training under your personal instructor, Do Jang owner, and the community of fellow members who are the Federation you have an opportunity to join the ranks of those who have achieved exceptional personal success.

Founder Hwang Kee stated that his original motivation for establishing the Moo Duk Kwan® in 1945 was to help human beings improve their internal power (Neh Gung), external power (Weh Gung) and mental/spiritual power (Shim Gung).

He expressed that such personal improvements would enable practitioners to improve their relationships with others and thus help them contribute a positive energy toward world peace through their study and practice of the unique Moo Duk Kwan® philosophy and the Soo Bahk Do® martial art system.

When the Federation's founding members structured the Federation, they did so based on Founder Hwang Kee's original intentions for his art that would assure the Federation's activity is properly recognized by United States law. In order to qualify for 501(c4) non-profit status, the IRS code states:

"To establish that your organization is organized exclusively for the promotion of social welfare, your organization must operate primarily in a way that furthers the common good and general welfare of the people of the community (such as bringing about civic betterment and social improvements in some way)."

The Federation's founding members knew that non-profit institutions do something very different than business or government and thus this was the motivation for establishing the Federation as non-profit entity.

Perhaps Founder Hwang Kee's personal life experiences with oppression and war in Korea at a very early age gave him a keen understanding of the unfortunate consequences of human conflict and helped him forge the Moo Duk Kwan® philosophy and discipline which he taught relentlessly his entire life (1945-2002). Perhaps those early experiences gave him a wisdom and insight well beyond his years which resulted in his vision for the Moo Duk Kwan® and its practitioners.

Whatever his reason, he has clearly stated that our Federation is, "to continue to develop as a 'Moo Do' organization while developing an atmosphere of respect, courtesy, friendship, brotherhood, cooperation, and goodwill that can help improve human relations worldwide and contribute to world peace."

This is the Mission we are charged with and which we must never forget.

As Federation members no one will make us do these things, rather our leaders will show us how to do these things and encourage us to follow their personal example. Only we can change ourselves and become an "action" oriented person or a "doer". These are the reasons why the Federation is a non-profit organization.

As a members' organization, your Federation depends heavily upon your membership dues to fund the ongoing and active pursuit of its Chartered Purposes, Mission 2000 and Vision Objectives. Without your financial support our cause would be lost.

Your voluntary participation in advanced member development programs such as instructor training programs, school ownership programs, events, and educational seminars also help fund the long-term preservation of Soo Bahk Do® as the most genuine of martial arts.

Individual membership support from every student is crucial to your Federation's cause and every member has a high opportunity to be an active advocate of the value of Federation membership to every parent, student, non-training Alumni, and the people in your community.

https://soobahkdo.com/about-usa-federation-membership/

WHAT IS THE UNITED STATES SOO BAHK DO MOO DUK KWAN FOUNDATION?

The United States Soo Bahk Do Moo Duk Kwan Foundation, Inc. is organized and operated as a 501c(3) non-profit organization solely and exclusively for charitable, educational and scientific purposes.

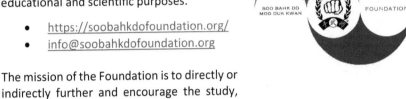

- https://soobahkdofoundation.org/
- info@soobahkdofoundation.org

The mission of the Foundation is to directly or indirectly further and encourage the study, the practice, and the growth of public recognition of the Soo Bahk Do® martial art system as licensed to do so by the United States Soo Bahk Do Moo Duk Kwan Federation, Inc.

The Foundation's initiatives include hosting educational seminars and events, distributing educational materials, literature, videos, etc. obtaining grants, soliciting donations, and other revenue sources that fund, through scholarships, donations and grants, or directly conducting community programs and cultural and educational activities to promote the Moo Duk Kwan® organization and the Soo Bahk Do® martial art system to help preserve its philosophy of conflict prevention, improving human relationships and moving toward world peace and harmony among all people.

The Foundation's goals include increasing public awareness of, and participation in, our Art. The Foundation also seeks to provide financial support to the Federation thus providing new participation opportunities to individuals who otherwise may not have an opportunity to experience our Art.

Should you wish to support the Foundation's initiatives by making a donation and increasing the number opportunities that the Foundation can offer, please visit www.soobahkdofoundation.org to make your donation. The Foundation has obtained tax exempt status from the IRS, which permits your donations to be tax deductible.

Your Federation's Structure

In 1975, Founder Hwang Kee and the Charter Members conceived and formed the U.S. Federation to promote the continued growth and public recognition of Soo Bahk Do® in the USA. The structure is organized as follows:

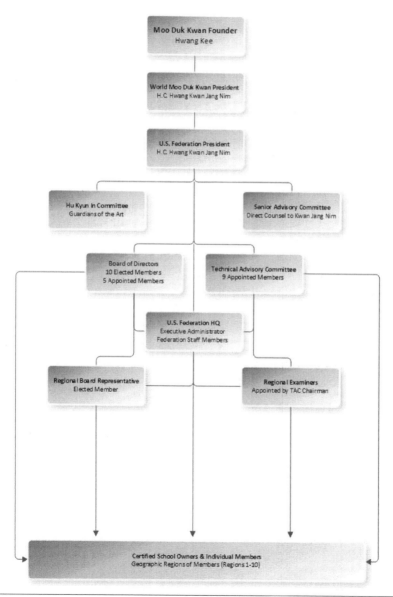

FEDERATION OFFICIALS

Senior Advisory Committee (S.A.C.)
The Senior Advisory Committee is comprised of senior Federation members appointed by the President to serve in an advisory and consultative capacity to the President in all matters he may deem appropriate.

Hu Kyun In (H.K.I.)
The Hu Kyun In is comprised of senior Federation members appointed by the President to maintain, preserve and perpetuate the History and Tradition of Soo Bahk Do® as taught in the Moo Duk Kwan®, sharing this knowledge and experience with the Members and with the greater community.

Technical Advisory Committee (T.A.C.)
The Technical Advisory Committee is comprised of Federation members appointed by the President to ensure that members have access to the technical guidance and insight needed to pursue study of the Moo Duk Kwan® curriculum for Soo Bahk Do® under your certified instructor. The Founder established very high standards for rank certification and for those who wish to be certified by the Moo Duk Kwan® to instruct Soo Bahk Do® to others. The T.A.C. is charged with upholding these standards throughout the Federation and with counseling the Board of Directors so that the activity of the Federation always preserves the purity and unique nature of our marital art.

Board of Directors (B.O.D.)
The business aspects and financial management of the Federation are vested in a board of directors. The Board of Directors consists of 15 Directors. Ten (10) are elected directors, with one elected from each geographic region defined in the bylaws and five (5) are directors appointed by the President.

Regional Examiners (R.E.X.)
Regional Examiners are appointed by the TAC Chairman to supervise and execute Regional Dan Shim Sa and other TAC activities in accordance with TAC and Board (Federation) guidelines. The volunteer Regional Examiners assist the TAC in coordinating School and Instructor Certifications, and providing regional members with technical training through special seminars. **Regional Administrators** provide business and administrative support for the Regional Examiners as well as supporting Regional Testing Boards and are typically selected by Regional Examiners and Senior Members of the Region and operate under the Board's authority with respect to business matters as expressed in Charter Article 4 Section 4&5.

Contacting Federation Headquarters & Officials

The Board of Directors and Technical Advisory Committee always encourage communication from all Federation members. Depending on the nature of your communication, it should be done in a manner that preserves and respects the "Moo Do" aspects of our Art.

If your inquiry is of a general nature or you wish to order educational materials or sales items, your Certified Instructor or Certified School Owner will most likely be able to handle your request, answer your question or direct you to who you should contact about your issue. In some cases, your Instructor may refer you to Headquarters or your Region's elected Board Director or one of your Regional Examiners for assistance. In most instances, you will be able to receive efficient, timely assistance through your local channels.

Any member experiencing anything less than excellent service and positive experiences as a Federation member is encouraged to communicate the issue of concern to the appropriate Federation representative.

National Member Headquarters
United States Soo Bahk Do Moo Duk Kwan Federation, Inc.
20 Millburn Ave Floor 2, Springfield, New Jersey 07081
- 9:00 AM to 5:00 PM. Eastern Time (Monday - Friday)
- Toll Free: 1-888-SOO-BAHK or (973) 467-3971
- Fax: 973-467-5716
- E-mail: headquarters@soobahkdo.com

Technical Advisory Committee (TAC)
If you require assistance concerning techniques, philosophy, history, or have a question regarding Individual Gup or Dan rank certification, Instructor Certification, or School Certification, please consult your Instructor or the Regional Examiner about the correct etiquette and then direct your communication to the Chairman of the Technical Advisory Committee.
- *E-Mail:* tacchair@soobahkdo.com

Board of Directors

Should you have questions about Federation programs, business policies or have an idea to submit you may communicate directly with your Elected Board Director within your Region or to the Chairman of the Board of Directors.

- *E-Mail:* boardchair@soobahkdo.com

Policy on Equal Opportunity, Affirmative Action and Harassment
By the Board of Directors

The commitment of the United States Soo Bahk Do Moo Duk Kwan Federation (referred hereafter as "the Federation") to the most fundamental principles of equality of opportunity and human dignity requires that decisions involving employees, volunteers, and members be based on individual merit and be free from invidious discrimination in all its forms.

It is the policy of the Federation not to engage in discrimination or harassment against any person because of race, color, religion, sex, national origin, ancestry, age, marital status, disability, sexual orientation, unfavorable discharge from the military, or status as a disabled veteran or veteran of the Vietnam era and to comply with all local, federal and state nondiscrimination, equal opportunity and affirmative action laws, orders and regulations.

This nondiscrimination policy applies to employment, access to and treatment in each Federation program and activity.

Mission 2000
By Founder Hwang Kee

Mission 2000 is a statement of goals or endpoints that comprises a vision of the global impact of the Moo Duk Kwan® and the Soo Bahk Do® martial art as expressed by Founder Hwang Kee.

It includes six objectives, endpoints or outcome statements or policies delivered to U.S. Federation members in 1989.

1. **Human Relationships (Internal - U.S.):** Continue to develop the atmosphere of respect, courtesy, friendship, brotherhood, cooperation, goodwill within the Soo Bahk Do Membership.

2. **Human Relationships (External - Global):** The atmosphere identified in number one should become consistent throughout the world.

3. **Moo Do Organization:** We are a martial (Moo Do) organization and we must continue to develop properly.

4. **Administration of the Organization:** The officers and the Board of Directors should take a more active role regarding the administration of the Federation.

5. **Members' Organization:** This is a members' organization. We must all work to produce a caring and helpful atmosphere for mutual benefit.

6. **Financial Stability:** We should take a more aggressive approach towards creating a financially stable organization.

BENEFITS OF FEDERATION MEMBERSHIP

- **Value of Membership**. Sa Bom Nim John Johnson, PhD eloquently conveys the value of being a Federation member, *"...This value can be categorized as:*
    a. *knowledge and skill;*
    b. *identity,*
    c. *authenticity and legitimacy;*
    d. *validity;*
    e. *credibility;*
    f. *institutional support; and,*
    g. *individual member support.*
  In short, the Federation is about the Moo Duk Kwan® organization and the Soo Bahk Do® martial art."

  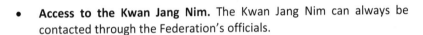

- **Access to the Kwan Jang Nim.** The Kwan Jang Nim can always be contacted through the Federation's officials.

- **World Moo Duk Kwan Affiliation**. As a Federation member, in addition to your USA national membership you are also automatically registered with the World Moo Duk Kwan® assuring that your rank certifications and instructor certifications are fully accredited by the World Moo Duk Kwan®.

- **International Relationships**. As a USA Federation member who is automatically registered with the World Moo Duk Kwan® you are eligible to participate in a host of activities in more than 23 countries.

- **Learn about the Five Moo Do Values**. Members have the opportunity to gain enlightenment about and understand each of the five Moo Do values and their significance in everyday life. The Federation seeks to apply those same values in all its activities and operations. *(History, Tradition, Discipline/Respect, Philosophy, Technique)*

- **Certification of Instructors and Schools.** Instructors and schools are certified by the Federation, assuring you that the instruction you receive at any Moo Duk Kwan® certified school will be the highest quality possible.

- **Background Check Approved Certified Instructors**. Effective 01/2019 the Board requires applicants for instructor certification over age 18 and certified instructors over age 18 to successfully pass a background check and complete specialized safety training course in order to apply for certification and/or maintain existing certification.

- **Educational Textbooks.** Textbooks and instructional guides written by Founder Hwang Kee and H.C. Hwang, are available for members and provide the most extensive analysis of Soo Bahk Do® in the world.

- **Moo Duk Kwan Mall.** Convenient online ordering for many items.

- **Moo Do Chul Hahk.** The Moo Do Chul Hahk (Moo Do Philosophy) presents a philosophy of the internationally recognized martial art grandmaster and Founder of the Moo Duk Kwan, Hwang Kee.

- **The Soo Bahk Do® Institute.** The Federation has constructed the world's largest and most comprehensive Moo Duk Kwan® video repository of Soo Bahk Do® instructional content. As of 2019 more than 1350 videos are available to subscribers covering forms, basic techniques, advanced techniques, other educational and historical content, demonstrations, testing performances and much, much more. Check your new member kit for a special subscription offer. https://www.soobahkdoinstitute.com/

- **Federation Wiki.** The Federation maintains a member editable wiki (like Wikipedia) featuring over 6000 pages of information about the organization, the art, resource links, member contributions and more.

- **Annual National Festival.** Members who gather at this premiere national event get to enjoy some of the best Soo Bahk Do® demonstrations and most highly skilled performances in the nation, meet old friends and make new friends.

- **Annual Ko Dan Ja Shim Sa.** Unique to the Moo Duk Kwan® and featured in National martial art publications, this eight-day experience is required of practitioners testing for 4th Dan and above.

- **Moment With The Masters.** Also unique to the Moo Duk Kwan®, those attending this annual weekend event get to train with the current year group of candidates testing for master level ranks and some of the most skilled Soo Bahk Do® instructors in the world.

- **Seminars, Workshops, and Camps.** Intensive instruction in forms, free sparring and more are available to all members.

- **Special Seminars.** The Technical Advisory committee makes seminars available which are taught by the Kwan Jang Nim, TAC members, Regional Examiners, SAC members, Hu Kyun In and senior instructors covering topics like the history, tradition, and philosophy of Soo Bahk Do® and technical content in order to provide members with an in-depth understanding of Soo Bahk Do® as taught in the Moo Duk Kwan®.

- **Publications.** The Federation publishes and distributes articles and media containing information about technical items, instructional tips and events. Members are invited to submit items to be considered for publication.

- **A Rich, Proud History.** As a member you will benefit from and share in the many historical accomplishments of Federation members before you and we encourage you to contribute to the collective, future accomplishments of the Moo Duk Kwan® and the USA Federation.
    a. You can learn much about the Federation's history in the historical issues of the Federation's printed newsletter archive:
        i. https://soobahkdo.com/federation-newsletter-archive/
    b. You can also access thousands of official Moo Duk Kwan® photos and articles dating back to 1945
        i. https://moodukkwanhistory.com/
    c. You can access oral history interviews from some of the most senior Moo Duk Kwan® members living and deceased recounting their first-hand experiences in the early years.
        i. https://oralhistory.soobahkdo.org/

- **Media Coverage.** The Federation publicizes Soo Bahk Do® in many different newspapers, magazines, and other appropriate media to promote our name and reputation.

- **Central Headquarters.** With a central office, you can get information, names and addresses of your old friends, and the location of other Soo Bahk Do® schools. You can also get definitive answers on matters of technique.

- **Official Moo Duk Kwan® apparel.** The Federation runs multiple time-limited apparel campaigns during the year when members can acquire official custom embroidered Moo Duk Kwan® apparel, gym bags, etc. and contribute to pursuit of the Federation's chartered purposes.

- <u>Visitation Rights</u>. If you are traveling, you will have the right to study at any Certified School. You must have permission from your instructor and gain permission from the schools you plan to visit. School information is available at: https://soobahkdo.com/locations/

- **Transfer between Schools.** If you move, the Federation can help locate the nearest member school and if you are an active member in good standing, your new school will recognize your current rank.

- **Standardization of Techniques.** The Technical Advisory Committee, assures that training is consistent throughout the country by providing national and regional seminars, clinics, books, films, and videos standardizing the practice of Soo Bahk Do®.

- **The Right to Hold Office and Vote.** Any member of the Federation 18 years and older, regardless of rank, can serve as a <u>Board Director</u> in the Federation. Dan members have the right to vote in Federation elections and charter revisions.

- **The Right to Be Heard.** As a member, you have the right to be heard and to petition Federation Officials concerning policies, problems, recommendations, compliments and good ideas. This can be done by through online means and by following the communication guidelines listed in this manual.
    a. https://soobahkdo.com/satisfaction/
    b. https://soobahkdo.com/testimonials/
    c. https://soobahkdo.com/idea-submission/
    d. https://soobahkdo.com/complaints/
    e. https://soobahkdo.com/reviews/

- **The Backing of the Federation.** As a member in good standing, if your credentials should ever be questioned, the Federation will back you with its full authority and cooperation.

- **Legitimacy.** As a member, you will belong to an organization that maintains the highest standards and that will not compromise itself, you, or the art of Soo Bahk Do®.

- **Growth and Sharing.** By attending the various functions, you will meet other members of the Federation, share your knowledge with them and vice versa, and develop friendships and relationships with fellow practitioners all over the United States and internationally.

- <u>Generous, Supportive Fellow Members</u>. Federation members generously support each other and numerous external causes. Founder Hwang Kee said *"Man is at his best when helping others, at his worst when bettering them."* <u>https://causes.soobahkdo.org/</u>

- <u>Leave a Legacy</u>. Federation members passionate about preserving the Soo Bahk Do® martial art for future generations can <u>create a personal legacy</u> that will live on in perpetuity via the organization. In addition to the Federation's non-tax deductible giving opportunities, the Federation's relationship with the United States Soo Bahk Do Moo Duk Kwan Foundation also makes tax-deductible opportunities available through a cooperative giving arrangement.

- <u>Complimentary Military Memberships</u>. The Federation provides free membership for all active U.S. military personnel (all branches and reserves) and their household members who enroll in a Certified School or Certified Teaching Program and submit a membership application in accordance with Federation guidelines effective September 1, 2011.

- <u>Charter</u> **and Authority of the Moo Duk Kwan® Founder and Kwan Jang Nim.** The Federation is the only organization in the United States chartered by and acting under the authority of the Moo Duk Kwan® Founder, Hwang Kee, and H.C. Hwang, Kwan Jang Nim. No other organization in the United States shall be recognized by the Founder or his successors.

- <u>Recommended Reading</u>. As a Federation member you have access to the minds and support of Kwan Jang Nim and all your fellow members in many ways including their personal recommendations about valuable reading materials.

Membership Code of Conduct
Charter Article 1 Section 3

Members shall follow the principles of Soo Bahk Do®:

1. Soo Bahk Do® is a classical martial art and not a sport. It is not a game to be played solely for the sake of winning, but rather a physical and intellectual activity designed to foster physical, mental, and spiritual health.
2. As a classical martial art, Soo Bahk Do® aims to develop and express the individual's true self, not the false self of aggrandizement.
3. As its major focus is on interior development, competition by groups or individuals is of minor usefulness in realizing individual potential.
4. Every practitioner of Soo Bahk Do® must do his or her utmost to retain the purity of this art and not debase it in any way.
5. People are at their best in helping others - at their worst in bettering others.
6. Every member shall: seek truth; work at developing their highest moral character; strive for humility; love their country; sacrifice himself/herself for justice; contribute, by example, to the acceptance of Soo Bahk Do® as the most genuine of the martial arts; develop their endurance; and value confidence and peace of mind.

Dues and Fees:

1. Members shall maintain dues, fees and charges current.
2. Members shall adhere to Administrative Responsibilities.

Set the Example:

- Members shall conduct themselves at all times as an example of what a proper martial artist should be (Moo Do Jaseh).
- The very fact that you study Soo Bahk Do® makes you an example of the state of the Art. This is a responsibility all members shall bear seriously and proudly.

REGIONAL STRUCTURE

The Federation's members are organized in 10 Regions that are geographically defined by the Board in Bylaws Article IV. *Note:* The letter next to the Region number corresponds with the member's Gup ID number.

- **Region 1 (A)**
    - Maine, New Hampshire, Vermont, Rhode Island, Massachusetts, Connecticut
- **Region 2 (B)**
    - New York, Pennsylvania, New Jersey, Maryland, Delaware, District of Columbia
- **Region 3 (C)**
    - Virginia, West Virginia, North Carolina, Tennessee, Kentucky, South Carolina
- **Region 4 (D)**
    - Florida, Georgia, Alabama, Mississippi, Louisiana, Puerto Rico, US Virgin Islands
- **Region 5 (E)**
    - Illinois, Indiana, Michigan, Ohio
- **Region 6 (F)**
    - Texas, Arkansas, Oklahoma, Kansas, Missouri
- **Region 7 (G)**
    - Minnesota, Iowa, Nebraska, South Dakota, North Dakota, Wisconsin
- **Region 8 (H)**
    - New Mexico, Arizona, Colorado, Utah, Wyoming, Idaho, Montana
- **Region 9 (I)**
    - Nevada, California, Hawaii
- **Region 10 (J)**
    - Oregon, Washington, Alaska

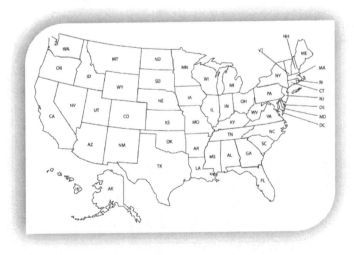

Opportunities of Federation Membership

Intellectual Property Use and Individual Members
Membership in the U.S. Federation confers full authority upon each individual member to study, train, seek rank certification in, seek instructor certification in, seek school certification in, promote public awareness of, and the practice of, the Moo Duk Kwan® and the Korean Soo Bahk Do® martial art system and to enjoy all the personal benefits associated therewith. However, individual members are not authorized to engage in commercial activities using the Soo Bahk Do® service marks or the Moo Duk Kwan® trademarks or any associated trademarks, service marks, logos or copyrighted content or materials.

Intellectual Property Use and Certified Instructors
Members are encouraged to explore and consider the rewards and opportunities of becoming a Certified Instructor and to explore the new opportunities for personal growth that come with being an instructor. Some members, who attain instructor certification, choose not to pursue school ownership as they find sufficient reward and enjoyment teaching in an existing school. Other members who attain instructor certification find teaching to be so rewarding and fulfilling that they also pursue school ownership in order to expand their opportunities for teaching and helping a greater number of people to benefit from training in the Soo Bahk Do® martial art system in their Moo Duk Kwan® certified school.

Intellectual Property Use and Certified Do Jang Owners
Members are encouraged to explore and consider the rewards and opportunities of school ownership (entrepreneurs) and ultimately seek school certification to teach the Soo Bahk Do® martial art system in their Moo Duk Kwan® certified school.

Members who become Certified School Owners receive authorization through the Federation to commercialize the instruction of the Soo Bahk Do® martial art system in accordance with Moo Duk Kwan® standards of excellence and in compliance with TAC and Board guidelines that assure preservation of the Moo Do attributes that make training in the Soo Bahk Do® martial art in a Moo Duk Kwan certified school such a unique experience.

Only members who attain school certification are granted authorization to engage in commercial activities using the Soo Bahk Do® martial art system service marks and Moo Duk Kwan® trademarks, service marks, logos and specific copyrighted content and materials.

The Federation is chartered as a non-profit organization and it reinvests its resources in promoting individual member development and the increasing public visibility of, study of and practice of Soo Bahk Do®. As such, the Kwan Jang Nim, the TAC, and the Board strongly encourage and support individual members who aspire to become school owners to prepare adequately, execute skillfully, and enjoy the rewarding experience of operating a "Successful Moo Do Do Jang" at whatever level fits with the member's life goals and dreams as a school owner.

Authentic, Legitimate Rank Certification

Authenticity differentiates the real from the imitation or forgery. Legitimacy differentiates what is authorized from what is not authorized.

This is the only organization in the United States that is recognized, authorized, and endorsed by the late Founder (Hwang Kee) and by H.C. Hwang Kwan Jang Nim of the Moo Duk Kwan®. Anyone else claiming to promote or train in Soo Bahk Do® or represent the Moo Duk Kwan® is a fraudulent imitation and illegitimate.

Authenticity and legitimacy are derived from a moral authority and primary source. The primary source and moral authority of the Soo Bahk Do® martial art and the Moo Duk Kwan® organization is derived directly from the Founder and Kwan Jang Nim or his successor. Without his acknowledgment and endorsement, there is no authenticity or legitimacy.

This is similar to every institutionalized authority. Without the recognition, acknowledgment, and endorsement of some agent that is acknowledged and recognized as a primary and legitimate authority and source, neither authenticity nor legitimacy can be inferred.

Since the United States Soo Bahk Do Moo Duk Kwan Federation® is the only organization in the United States authorized and recognized by the Kwan Jang Nim, membership in this organization is the only legitimate means of practicing and training in the martial art of Soo Bahk Do® as taught in Moo Duk Kwan® schools. It also legitimizes all certifications and ranks awarded.

School (Do Jang) Ownership Opportunities

Motivated members who want to take their passion for Soo Bahk Do® to an even higher level and help change even more people's lives in a positive way and make a bigger difference in their community and the world are invited to explore the rewards and opportunities of Moo Duk Kwan® certified Do Jang ownership.

Only a very few high achieving members have the additional traits, characteristics, drive, and determination that make a "Successful Moo Do Do Jang" owner and for those who do, nothing can stand in their way.

Do Jang ownership can take many forms depending on your life goals and aspirations. Some members with professional careers and a well-established life find personal reward in offering a small, part-time program in their church, Y.M.C.A., recreation center, etc.

Some younger members discover opportunities to teach Soo Bahk Do Moo Duk Kwan programs in their church, local community groups, schools, etc.

Teens and graduating high school students planning to pursue vocational careers after high school discover that their passion for Soo Bahk Do® provides more rewarding opportunities for them than the vocational career they may have originally targeted.

Young adults going off to college may choose to initiate a part-time Soo Bahk Do® program as their part-time job instead of working in other typical jobs that college students often hold.

Some members later in life may leave the corporate world behind to pursue the unmatched personal rewards of changing people's lives and making a profound difference in their community and the world by pursuing the exciting challenges and entrepreneurial opportunities of Moo Duk Kwan® certified Do Jang ownership.

Some members operate non-profit programs that serve communities of students with special needs and others offer non-profit programs in school districts and more.

Some members start out teaching a part-time program and as their student body grows over time, they discover that the personal rewards of teaching and operating their Do Jang exceed the rewards of their day job and eventually convert from a part-time Do Jang owner to a full-time Moo Duk Kwan® certified Do Jang owner.

Whatever your life goals and your level of passion for teaching Soo Bahk Do® and integrating it into your life, the Federation stands ready to help prepare you and support you in achieving your dreams.

INTERNATIONAL GOODWILL OPPORTUNITIES

The World Moo Duk Kwan® periodically issues invitations to U.S. Federation members to participate in various international events, activities and proceedings.

Members of all ranks are invited to explore international training opportunities unless a particular activity is published as rank specific or limited to specific invitees. (i.e. World Moo Duk Kwan Symposium)

Members are requested to observe World Moo Duk Kwan international Visitation Protocol when making plans to travel or train internationally.

World Moo Duk Kwan international events are posted for member awareness on the calendars at www.soobahkdo.com and www.worldmoodukkwan.com.

U.S. Federation members are encouraged to exhibit full support of Mission 2000 directives with special attention to improving human relations at home and abroad.

The U.S. Federation extends substantial Goodwill support to the World Moo Duk Kwan in the spirit of Mission 2000 and in accordance with the Charter & Bylaws and Board Governance Policies.

Youth Leadership Program

What is the Youth Leadership Program?

The Youth Leadership Program provides an opportunity for practioners up to age 25 to connect with each other through Moo Do activities. The lasting bonds created through training and social experiences will strengthen the Moo Do identity of the youth members and groom the next generation of Moo Duk Kwan® leaders.

Who is eligible?

All youth members are eligible to participate in different ways.

Event Type	Title	Events	Ranks	Age	Appointed By
Local (Do Jang) Events	Youth Leader	Special Training: Board Breaking, Hyung, History, Parties, etc..	All Ranks	All Ages	Instructor
Regional Events	Youth Leader / Do Jang Rep.	Youth training tracks, demonstrations, youth gatherings	All Ranks	10-25	Instructor
National Events	Regional Rep.	- National Festival: Annual Youth Demonstration, Youth Leadership Training Tracks, Regional Rep. Meetings - Moment with the Masters: Exclusive Youth Leadership Training Tracks	1st Dan to 4th Dan	13-25	Regional Examiner
International Events	National Rep.	- WMDK Youth Leadership Symposium in Korea - Connect with Youth Leaders at International Events	3rd Dan to 4th Dan	18-25	Technical Advisory Committee

Why is it important?

Identifying Youth Leaders in your school will help members take pride and ownership of their Moo Do journey. It will highlight passionate members and give their juniors something to aspire to. Youth Leaders will make friendships along the way and build the foundation for future generations of Moo Duk Kwan® leaders.

Mission Statement

- To preserve the Moo Duk Kwan® as created by Founder, Hwang Kee.
- To seek to strengthen and promote the global identity of Moo Duk Kwan® through social media and in our daily lives.
- To encourage and strengthen the international relationships among the youth to support the development of the Moo Duk Kwan®.
- To promote the longevity of the Moo Duk Kwan® by supporting and empowering the leaders of tomorrow.

World Moo Duk Kwan® Youth Leadership Videos

Criteria for each video is different and is determined by the WMDK Youth Leadership Program (YLP) Video Committee. This committee is comprised of National Representatives currently serving their National organization. The criteria for each video will be announced by the TAC Jin Heung Bu and they will determine which videos will be included on behalf of the USA. All eligible youth are encouraged to participate. Submissions will be made to the WMDK YLP Video Committee via the TAC Jin Heung Bu and final selections will be made by the WMDK YLP Video Committee.

World Moo Duk Kwan® Youth Leadership Symposium in Korea

This annual event is a special opportunity for Youth Leaders from across the globe to train with each other and discuss developments in their countries. The National Representative will be selected by the TAC and will receive room and board for the weeklong symposium. Other Youth Leaders may participate at their own expense with TAC approval.

Vision Objectives: "A Living Art; Living the Art"
By H.C. Hwang, Kwan Jang Nim

We have clearly identified our Five Moo Do values: History, Tradition, Philosophy, Discipline/Respect, and Technique, as being the foundation of our identity.

I am proud of being a Moo Duk Kwan Jeh Ja and am grateful to our Founder, Hwang Kee for the cultural inheritance that he left for us all. In order for us to honor, protect, and preserve the gift we have received, we must seek to polish it to its highest shine for all to see and take every possible action to ensure its longevity. I believe these goals will be achieved naturally as we strengthen the Five Moo Do values (our inheritance) within each one of us, through our thoughts and our actions.

We, as Moo Duk Kwan practitioners, have a tremendous opportunity to influence our communities and our society in many positive ways as we further embrace and practice the Five Moo Do values in our behaviors. Such unique behavior will certainly attract the attention of our communities and as they increasingly recognize us, the doors of Moo Duk Kwan Do Jang will be opened wider than ever to their communities. Your Do Jang must be highly visible as a "Successful Moo Do Do Jang" in your communities. **The Moo Duk Kwan needs your active participation.**

As we continue to strengthen ourselves based on the 5 Moo Do Values, we can measure our progress toward creating a "Successful Moo Do Do Jang" and assuring the long-term preservation of Soo Bahk Do Moo Duk Kwan in two important ways:

1. By sharing our success stories about how our application of the 5 Moo Do values in our actions positively impacted others in our community. Inspirational success stories help reinforce our self-awareness of the many opportunities each of us have to improve our behaviors based on the values.
2. By increasing student enrollment through the successful application of the concepts conveyed in the Vision Tour. Increased membership in the Do Jang provides measurable evidence of our success at connecting our values with our communities. Increased membership in the Federation confirms our success at connecting more people in our society with our values.

A truly "Successful Moo Do Do Jang" must accomplish items 1 and 2, not just 1 or 2. Achieving both requires more than just the instructor's effort. It requires the involvement, support and active outreach into the community by every student, assistant, parent, friend and relative who supports our values.

On July 29, 2005, Moo Duk Kwan members (about 50) and I attended the 2005 Black Belt Hall of Fame Award Banquet in Hollywood, California. After experiencing that evening, I came to realize how very far we have come and appreciate our success as a quality Moo Do organization.

I have never been more proud and appreciative of the Moo Duk Kwan's members than at that time and now. All 50 Moo Duk Kwan members who were present shared the same experience that evening and for me it was really an "awakening" moment to see that we truly are the leading Martial Art group in the World.

For too long we have been too quiet about our values. This is the time to celebrate our values and raise the volume of our voices for others to hear. It is time to demonstrate our values through our "Successful Moo Do Do Jang." It is time to achieve 1 and 2.

When you believe in the values and are passionate about sharing them with others through your actions, they can be positively contagious within your community. I invite you to join me in accomplishing these 2 important goals for our art and its future.

Thank you for your continued support of our art and I shall look forward to your energetic support for increasing the visibility of our art and assuring its long-term preservation.

YOUR PERSONAL TRAINING EXPERIENCE
"There Is Only One Moo Duk Kwan®"

Hwang Kee,
Moo Duk Kwan Founder
1914-2002

Although unknown by some Tae Kwon Do, Tang Soo Do, Soo Bahk Do®, and other martial art practitioners who may be displaying the Moo Duk Kwan® name or the fist emblem commonly associated with it, all have a common history.

The fist emblem first existed only in the mind of unknown Hwang Kee (Founder) who was born November 9, 1914 during Japan's occupation of Korea. At age seven he witnessed a lone man successfully defend himself against seven attackers using martial arts techniques referred to by onlookers as "Tae Kyun" or "Sip Pal Ki" and from that day forward he dedicated his life to developing skills like those he had observed. His unflagging pursuit of prowess in the martial arts earned him a reputation as a martial arts prodigy and although Japanese rule prohibited it, he dreamed of someday opening his own martial arts training hall where he could teach others. His dream became a reality shortly after the Japanese occupation of Korea ended and his first Moo Duk Kwan® (Military Virtue Institute/Training Hall) Do Jang opened on November 9, 1945.

In his Moo Duk Kwan® he offered instruction in his unique martial art system named "Hwa Soo Do" and in May 1949 he published Hwa Soo Do Kyo Bohn, the first modern martial arts book published in Korea. Soon he realized that if his art was to flourish wider public recognition was necessary. So he adopted the more recognizable name of "Tang Soo Do" and public demand quickly created Moo Duk Kwan® training halls all across Korea.

After 1953 when the Korean War ended, the United States military personnel who trained in Korea began returning to the United States, where they were soon teaching his martial art system to students in the United States. Within a few years he conceived and designed his unique fist logo to publicly identify his Moo Duk Kwan® training halls as the only source of official training and rank certification in his martial art system and to symbolize his art's philosophy. Hwang Kee's fist emblem was quickly and passionately embraced and displayed by proud Moo Duk Kwan® practitioners worldwide to indicate that they embraced the Moo Duk Kwan's® strong identity, its scientific and effective martial art system and its philosophy.

By 1960 Hwang Kee had incorporated new material into his "living art" and adopted the name "Soo Bahk Do®" to emphasize and publicize his Moo Duk Kwan's® commitment to resurrecting Korea's culture and preserving its lost martial arts history that he had discovered in the text "Moo Yei Do Bo Tong Ji." His fist emblem soon became deeply embedded in Korean practitioners' hearts and minds as a symbol of Korea's pride in its new emerging identity as an independent nation and in a culture that was finally, truly Korean.

Moo Yei Do Bo Tong Ji

The Moo Duk Kwan® experienced tremendous success and widespread public appeal which attracted government interest in the martial arts and in 1964 the Korean Tae Kwon Do Association was formed to unite all Korea martial artists under one name and eliminate individual kwans. Under tremendous political pressure, Hwang Kee resolutely insisted upon preserving the unique identity of the Moo Duk Kwan® and his martial art system and he successfully fought a legal battle to maintain the right to do so all the way to the Korean Supreme Court in June 1966. By this time the fracturing of Moo Duk Kwan® members was well underway due to mounting political pressures and competing loyalties; but interestingly, almost all who forfeited their ties with the Moo Duk Kwan® and its founder steadfastly continued their use and proud display of his fist emblem and the Moo Duk Kwan® name. Even as many succumbed to political pressures and adopted the Tae Kwon Do name, they refused to relinquish their use of Hwang Kee's fist emblem due to their strong emotional investment in, and attachment to, all that it symbolizes.

In 1987 The Founder Hwang Kee trademarked his fist emblem in the United States in order to curtail public misrepresentation by parties who were no longer affiliated with his Moo Duk Kwan®.

Even today, some practitioners still display The Founder Hwang Kee's fist emblem without knowledge of its origin, its meaning, its rich history and without awareness that only current members of the Moo Duk Kwan® are legally authorized to display it in honor of The Founder Hwang Kee's legacy to the world.

His fist emblem has come to represent the spirit of an undefeatable warrior and a dedicated scholar. That which it represents has proven to be far more resilient and powerful than all the forces that have besieged it since its inception.

Founder Hwang Kee's heart, spirit and legacy truly live on in the fist image that he created to represent the essence of his life's work.

All who display it are the children of his life.

- *By Phil Duncan, Sa Bom based on information from the textbook, "History of the Moo Duk Kwan" by The Founder Hwang Kee and   H.C. Hwang Kwan Jang Nim.*

THE FIVE MOO DO VALUES

By H.C. Hwang Kwan Jang Nim

The Five Moo Do values of History, Tradition, Philosophy, Discipline/Respect, and Technique, are the backbones of our proud Moo Do identity. These values coexist interdependently with each element strengthening the meaning of the other four. When we apply the Five Moo Do values to our daily training, we strengthen our self not only as a Moo Do practitioner, but also as an individual who provides a positive influence within our society. I trust this discussion of our Five Moo Do Values will help Moo Duk Kwan® practitioners to include them in all aspects of your life as basic action elements in your behaviors rather than just being concepts to speak about.

History (Yuk Sa)

"History is a chronological record of significant events (as affecting.... an institution) often including an explanation of their cause" (Webster's Ninth New Collegiate Dictionary <1989>).

These events, causes and the individuals involved, become the second heavenly nature of the institution/organization/concept.

History defines us. We understand who we are by knowing our history (past). This knowledge helps guide our actions with an awareness of our foundation, our history, our past, and helps us understand where we are in the present as we create our future.

Our history (past) is the guiding source for our future life. We can create our future by honoring our history (past). The experiences of our elders, seniors and instructors are part of our past, so we honor (respect) them because they created the foundation upon which our present has been built and their experiences serve as a guiding source for creating our future.

We can benefit from listening, valuing, and respecting their teachings and the wisdom they share with us about their experiences.

Consider some visible behaviors that we can initiate to put our history into our actions:
- We can concede our seat to elders or provide them with assistance such as carrying a heavy object for them, etc.
- We can listen to and honor our parents and grandparents (elders) advice and counsel.
- We can listen to our teachers and apply the knowledge they share with us.
- We can demonstrate good academic behavior.

History will help strengthen our respect. We will become better learners and students as a result. "Loyalty" (Choong) is one of the most important words in the Moo Do world.

Regretfully, loyalty is often motivated by a desire for a position, power, or money. However, this type of insincere loyalty will not last when the position, power, or money situation changes. Individuals who have failed in their loyalty often seek to hide their past.

Loyalty, commitment: the act of binding yourself (intellectually or emotionally) to a course of action; a prime virtue, unswerving in allegiance, and implies a faithfulness that is steadfast in the face of any temptation to renounce, desert, or betray.

If loyalty is established based upon History, then loyalty will never change because the History upon which it is built will never change. Consider some additional behaviors that we can initiate to put our History into our actions.

- We can be a good example (human story) by upholding our loyalty as demonstrated through our behavior even during difficult situations. People learn from and appreciate our example (story).
- We can be loyal to a principle rather than to that which is convenient or rewarding.
- We can honor techniques that were built upon a true historical background.
- History strengthens Tradition, Philosophy, Discipline/Respect, and Technique.

- Do my behaviors reflect my history? Do my actions demonstrate and honor my history?

Tradition (Jun Tong)

"Tradition is that which is inherited, established, or transmitted and passed on as a customary pattern of thought, action, or behavior; the handing down of information, beliefs, and customs…" (Ibid).

This is the process by which the essence of Soo Bahk Do® Moo Duk Kwan® is maintained.

There are traditional means of conduct and beliefs which were handed down since the inception of the Moo Duk Kwan®. Some originated even before the Moo Duk Kwan®. These traditions began at some point in history. The tradition of bowing is a show of respect and/or appreciation.

Once upon a time as students were receiving instruction from a teacher and were enlightened from the instruction of their teacher, their overwhelming happiness may have motivated them to lower their body in order to look up to their teacher in respect for, and appreciation of, their teacher. This could have been the birth of the bowing tradition. Since that time, students' desire to celebrate and remember the spirit of learning, respect and appreciation have been preserved through the tradition of bowing to the teacher. The bow has become a tradition to show the spirit of joy, respect and appreciation. The bowing tradition carries on this spirit.

Can you imagine if they did not share the bow after that? There would be no spirit of respect and appreciation. There is no life of learning if there is no spirit.

Perhaps you recall a particular moment (playing cards or sharing a particular brand of drink etc.,) when you established a friendship with someone. You may recreate that special moment of the birth of your friendship from time to time as a tradition to celebrate the spirit of the moment when your friendship was first born. Your friendship will be strengthened, healthy and full of spirit when you keep that tradition in your meetings. However, your friendship may suffer or diminish should you neglect the tradition.

Our traditions strengthen our spirits and create a positive influence and connection with the other four Moo Do Values.

Consider these two families and the traditions in their lives. The Smith family celebrated a holiday by decorating their house and selecting costumes and candy as they prepared weeks beforehand in the spirit of the holiday.

The children were having a joyful experience during this time and were filled with excitement and hope about the coming festivities. The Smith family members and their neighbors became closer and their relationship was strengthened through these traditions which had a very positive effect upon human relationships.

The Tom family was too busy and tired to prepare for the holiday and chose to just watch television instead of observing the traditions of the holiday because doing so would require work. Their home and family members showed no holiday spirit and the children had no reason to be excited or filled with anticipation.

Traditions in action are visible in:
- Those who are hardworking people.
- Those who carry high spirits.
- Those who lead the way (initiative).
- Those who honor and perform rituals and techniques that embrace habits from past generations.
- Do my actions preserve my traditions?
- Do my behaviors embody my traditions?

Philosophy (Chul Hak)

"Philosophy is a set of ideas or beliefs relating to a particular field or activity; an underlying theory, a system of values by which one lives; the most general beliefs, concepts, and attitudes of an individual or group..." (Ibid).

Our philosophy guides our intent (Shim Gung) toward the good.

Our philosophy includes the 8 Key Concepts, the 10 Articles of Faith on Mental Training, and many other ideas and values. Our active study of these tools and our application of them as a Moo Duk Kwan practitioner strengthens our life and demonstrates the philosophy we live by.

In training, our first Shi Sun is an action of intent. Our intent is much clearer when it is based upon our philosophy. We experience a good class for both your mind and body when our intent is clear.

When Peter greets his instructor upon arriving at the Do Jang and again when he leaves the Do Jang, then his courteous behavior may also extend into his life beyond the Do Jang. It becomes a good foundation for him to build human relations through his behavior. Peter's intent was strengthened by the Jhoon Bee philosophy "start good, finish good."

Philosophy strengthens Discipline and Respect.
- Our intent guides our actions.
- Our actions will be meaningful when they are initiated with good intent.

These are some visible behavioral measurements of philosophy in action:
- The person whose philosophy is demonstrated by their actions rather than talk.
- The person who is providing views based on the principle.
- The person who makes a decision based on the principle.
- Does my behavior demonstrate our philosophy?

Discipline / Respect (Ki Khang / Jon Kyung)

"Discipline is the study, or practice, of a subject using a specific set of methods, terms and approaches..." (Ibid)

"Respect is the objective, unbiased consideration and regard for the rights, values, beliefs and property of all people; deference and courteous regard for people's feelings..." (Ibid)

Discipline and respect are the foundation of the Human relations.

Discipline will strengthen your professional conduct. Respect will strengthen your kindness. Discipline alone may bring the hard side which makes others uncomfortable. Respect alone may bring the soft side which makes others overly comfortable. These factors alone will bring a negative influence on human relations. Discipline and respect should coexist with each other to gain their full benefit for human relations. Furthermore, they should be strengthened by the other four Moo Do values in order to fulfill their meaning. In other words, Professionalism (Discipline) and Kindness (Respect) alone are not what we strive for in the Moo Do world. In the end, they will be nothing more than sales tactics. Alone, they may merely be the tools for "people skills" that sales representatives use at stores.

Professionalism (Discipline) and Kindness (Respect) must be strengthened by History, Tradition, Philosophy, and Technique in order to fulfill their true values. These are some of the visible behavioral measurements of discipline in action:
- Professional conduct rather than casual demeanor
- Proper postures (ways of standing and sitting posture)
- Dependability

These are some of the visible behavioral measurements of respect in action:
- Helping and caring for others
- Smile, kindness
- Recognition
- Carrying proper body mannerism with care and politeness

While we respect individualism, providing visual demonstrations of body images that reflect discipline and respect in the class can be helpful to connect our thoughts of respect to our body mannerisms.

- Do I have discipline in my behavior? Do I have respect in my behavior?

Technique (Ki Sul)

"Technique is the manner in which technical details are treated or as basic physical movements are used..."(Ibid) Techniques are very visible elements of Soo Bahk Do Moo Duk Kwan.

We gain the benefits of flexibility, self-defense skills, and health as we train to improve our techniques.

Techniques from Gi Cho, Hyung, and Dae Ryun are excellent tools for connecting with the other four Moo Do Values, History, Tradition, Philosophy, and Discipline/Respect. From this connection we benefit by strengthening our techniques.

Seeking to apply all our Moo Do values during our technical performance of techniques helps us to understand the relationships between our techniques and the other four Moo Do Values.
Techniques when performed based upon History, Tradition, Philosophy, and Discipline/Respect will develop beyond just physical techniques.

When we perform Soo Gi or Jok Gi techniques with good Huh Ri extension, connect our value of using Huh Ri to our unique identity as a Moo Duk Kwan practitioner. Our identity as well as our technique is strengthened.

When we perform "Jang Kap Kwon Kong Kyuk" or "Yuk Ro/Chil Sung Hyung", we are connecting with the values of History (and/or Philosophy) of Soo Bahk Do Moo Duk Kwan and they will become more than techniques.

By training in our Techniques and applying the guidelines of the 5 Moo Do Values, our training becomes a freedom that provides new realization, understanding and creativity. We become connected not only to the art's history, but we also become the foundation of the art's future creativity. Through this process, both History and Philosophy will be strengthened.

When we perform a traditional ceremony during our training (bowing with Sa Bom Nim or partner) and we connect with the meaning and spirit of our bow, then our Moo Do Spirit (Moo Do Chung Shin) becomes fuller and will guide our training to the fullest.

When we connect Discipline/Respect to our training, then our techniques and attitudes become more effective and enjoyable. We can seek to enjoy the application of Discipline and Respect in our training and both will be strengthened as a result.

Consider these visible behaviors that demonstrate our Techniques in Action:
- Techniques are visible things, therefore they can be seen and measured.
- Punching and kicking are not the only techniques that we consider. Any kind of physical presentation can be considered as technique in this discussion. For example:
    o What kind of mannerism is appropriate when I visit my teacher?
    o What is appropriate when I am challenged by someone etc.?
    o How do I approach, respond, to and behave based on different circumstance?

Mental and Physical mannerisms which are strengthened by the 5 Moo Do values can be the most powerful techniques we may possess.

These mannerisms give you an ability not only to defend yourself but also to build toward a peaceful world.

The Eight Key Concepts
By H.C. Hwang, Kwan Jang Nim

용기	Yong Gi	Courage
정신통일	Chung Shin Tong Il	Concentration
인내	In Neh	Endurance
정직	Chung Jik	Honesty
겸손	Kyum Son	Humility
힘조정	Him Cho Chung	Control of Power
신축	Shin Chook	Tension Relaxation
완급	Wan Gup	Speed Control

One of the aspects of the Mission 2000 agenda for the U.S. Federation is that we should strive to be a "Moo Do Organization". As a Moo Duk Kwan Dan member or instructor, one way to contribute to achieving this goal is to take action so that our Moo Duk Kwan philosophy connects with students. This implies that our instruction has to connect with Moo Duk Kwan philosophy as effectively as possible.

This article discusses the incorporation of the philosophy of the Eight Key Concepts into Moo Duk Kwan instruction. The motivation for this article stems from reviewing and meditating on the many Cho Dan Shim Sa essays submitted over the years by Il Gup who were candidates for Cho Dan. Although individuals expressed it in variety of different personal ways, almost 100% of the Cho Dan candidates discuss Moo Duk Kwan philosophy in their essay. In fact, from reading these essays it was clear that the Moo Duk Kwan philosophy for them was the strongest source of motivation for continuing their training. Invariably they relate their experience and the value of their training in some way to Moo Duk Kwan philosophy -- especially the "Eight Key Concepts" and/or the "Ten Articles of Faith on Mental Training" in their Cho Dan essays.

The Cho Dan candidates discuss how the Moo Duk Kwan philosophy has influenced their lives for the better, and how it has provided them with a strong sense of dedication -- a strong positive influence that contributed very much to their continued Soo Bahk Do training. It is a pleasure to see that our membership puts the value of philosophy in a high place in their study of Soo Bahk Do Moo Duk Kwan.

Since the Eight Key Concepts have provided such a profound impact and motivation to practitioners who have achieved Cho Dan level, then perhaps for those that do not reach Cho Dan level -- they may not have been sufficiently exposed to the 8 Key Concepts. Perhaps the motivation and value of the Eight Key Concepts may not have been introduced and/or reinforced as effectively as they could have been.

If we, in our role as instructors, could improve on how we introduce the Eight Key Concepts – making sure every student receives a proper introduction to the Key Concepts at the appropriate stage of their training and continue to reinforce them as a regular part of their instruction, it will prove to be very beneficial. If we can accomplish this, then we could help provide a much more positive influence on Yu Gup Ja. This impact would not only have immediate benefits for the students, but would also be a lasting influence throughout their future Moo Do training.

For instructors, this is not an easy task. As instructors, we need to discipline ourselves to focus on instruction of the Eight Key Concepts and take advantage of opportunities to reinforce them. If we are effective, then we will stay better connected with our students and they would not miss the experience and value of the education provided by the Key Concepts.

Ten Articles of Faith on Mental Training

1. **Be loyal to your country**; sacrifice yourself for your duty to your country and your people. This is based on the spirit of the Hwa Rang.
2. **Be obedient to your parents**; children should be dutiful to your parents and parents should be charitable to their children.
3. **Be loving between husband and wife**; love and affection between the sexes develops mankind's happiness and harmony in life.
4. **Be cooperative between brothers**; hold together with cooperation and concord.
5. **Be respectful to your elders**; protect the rights of the weak with courtesy and modesty.
6. **Be faithful between teacher and student**; learn the truth through practice of duty and affection.
7. **Be faithful between friends**; be peaceful and happy with harmony and faith towards each other, regardless of race, and towards all mankind.
8. **Face combat only in justice and with honor**; be able to distinguish between good and bad with fairness and rightfulness.
9. **Never retreat in battle**; sacrifice for justice with capability and bravery.
10. **Always finish what you start**; move to action with sureness and hope.

5 Requirements & 11 Points of Emphasis on Mental Training

Requirements
1. Oneness with Nature
2. Complete Awareness with Environment
3. Experience
4. Conscience
5. Culture

Emphasis
1. Reverence for Nature
2. Physical Control (Ki Hap)
3. Courtesy
4. Modesty
5. Thankfulness
6. Self-Sacrifice
7. Courage
8. Chastity
9. Strength Inside and Mildness Outside
10. Endurance
11. Reading Ability

5 Requirements & 10 Points of Emphasis on Physical Training

Requirements
1. Contact with Physical Surroundings
2. Contact with Diverse Physical Conditions
3. Suitable Nourishment
4. Suitable Exercise
5. Suitable Rest

Emphasis
1. Vocal Exhalation for Thoracic Strength (Ki Hap)
2. Focus of Sight
3. Continuous Balance during Movement
4. Flexibility of the Body
5. Correct Muscle Tone for Maximum Power
6. High and Low Speed Technique
7. Exactness of Technique
8. Adjustment for Proper Distance
9. Proper Breathing for Endurance
10. Conditioning of Hands and Feet

Guidelines for Training

Approach your Soo Bahk Do® training with an open mind. Remember that the goals and purpose of this martial art are not the same as a sport. Note these 10 specific attributes that characterize the Soo Bahk Do® martial art:

1. It is natural and reasonable to practice a martial art.
2. It is non-restrictive and expresses freedom of movement.
3. It combines civil and military arts that are both strong and submissive.
4. It is good practice for mental and physical well-being.
5. It is good for self-defense and improvement of personal health.
6. You can practice as an individual or as a member of a group.
7. You can practice anywhere.
8. Anyone can learn with a little effort and faith, regardless if they are man, woman, elderly, or young.
9. You can practice whether you have a partner or not.
10. You don't need any instruments or special equipment to practice with.

When we train in Soo Bahk Do®, we do not face a "game" or contest, but physical, mental, and spiritual interaction between ourselves and our art. As such, the benefit that one gains from this practice is immediate and enduring. Whether we meet an outside challenge or face our own weaknesses, we build our character on a strong foundation of discipline, replacing the temporary situation of victory or defeat with the lasting benefits of greater self-esteem and self-confidence.

The Founder reminded us, through his teachings, that we must not forget our place in the world. Soo Bahk Do® practitioners must harmonize their existence within nature and human society. Note the 5 requirements and 11 Points of Emphasis on Mental Training.

Hyung (Forms) Training Discipline

- Hyung training is both a mental and physical discipline.
- Concentration is essential.
- Every attempt at a Hyung requires and should involve maximum effort.
- Perfection requires continuous practice.
- You are perpetuating the art and you represent the way of Soo Bahk Do
- In learning a new Hyung
    - Learn the origin and characteristics, and then memorize the sequence.
    - Study the application and cultivate awareness of body posture and the external situation.
    - Concentrate on breath control, tension, relaxation, power, and intent.
    - Take on the mental significance and Soo Bahk Do meaning of the Hyung.
- Never attempt a form without the advice and consent of your instructor.
- Patience is as important as physical ability in developing a perfect Hyung.
- Develop your own psychological technique for overcoming idleness, inertia, distractions, and mental blocks.
- After practice, learn to relax and to appreciate the gains you have made, no matter how small.

Uniform & Belts

The uniform or training suit is properly called Do Bok. This is a composite word, combining Do "way of life" with Bok "apparel" or "clothing." Since the Do Bok is what you wear when you practice your "Do" or way, its care and meaning are very important.

Similarities can be found between the current Do Bok and ancient Korean traditional clothing. Today, we maintain the white color to show purity, reverence for life, and commitment to avoiding bloodshed and violence.

Action and thought are inseparable. Also, the outside appearance and inside attitude are closely linked. When you look your best, you usually feel good, too.

Keeping this in mind, always appear in class with your uniform clean and pressed, in good repair, and with the proper trim for your rank. Your Instructor or seniors will help instruct you in the proper care and wearing of your Do Bok.

Gup Belt and Uniform Requirements

Rank	Belt with Stripes on Tip	Uniform and Trim Color
10th Gup	White Belt	White – no trim
9th Gup	White Belt – one blue strip	White – no trim
8th Gup	Orange Belt	White – no trim
7th Gup	Orange Belt – one blue strip	White – no trim
6th Gup	Green Belt	White – green lapel trim
5th Gup	Green Belt – one blue stripe	White – green lapel trim
4th Gup	Green Belt – two blue stripes	White – green lapel trim
3rd Gup	Red Belt	White – red lapel trim
2nd Gup	Red Belt – one blue stripe	White – red lapel trim
1st Gup	Red Belt – two blue stripes	White – red lapel trim

NOTE:
- Midnight blue stripes on Gup rank belts are to be on the left end of the belt approximately 2" from the tip of the belt.
- Stripes are to be 1/2" wide and 1/2" apart.
- Gup lapel trim shall cover the lapel binding (approximately 1 3/4").
- White and Orange belt Gup rank students shall not trim uniform jackets.
- Green and Red belt Gup rank students shall have uniform jackets with trim on lapel only.

Dan Belt and Uniform Requirements

Rank	Belt with Stripes on Tip	Uniform and Trim color
1st Dan	Midnight Blue Belt	White uniform with midnight blue trim on - Lapel - Sleeve cuffs - Bottom jacket hem
2nd Dan	Midnight Blue Belt with Two white stripes	
3rd Dan	Midnight Blue Belt with Three white stripes	
4th to 9th Dan	Midnight Blue Belt with Red stripe in center of belt, all around	

NOTE:
- All white stripes on Dan rank belts are to be on the left end of the belt approximately 2" from the tip of the belt.
- Stripes are to be 1/2" wide and 1/2" apart.
- Dan lapel trim shall cover the lapel binding (approximately 1 3/4 ").
- Dan members shall have trimmed uniform jackets, which include lapel, sleeve cuffs, and all around the bottom border.

Meaning of the Belt Colors

- Colors in the Moo Duk Kwan flag are the same as those used in the belt ranking system.

Color	Season	Meaning
White	Winter	Emptiness, innocence, hidden potential, purity
Orange	Between Winter & Spring	Orange was officially added in 1975, under the Grandmaster's approval, as an extra step between white and green belts.
Green	Spring	Growth, advancement
Red	Summer	Ripening, "Yang", active
Blue	Autumn	Harvest, maturity, "Um", passive

The Flags

On the wall of your Do Jang (school), you will see three flags.
- The one on the left is the American flag.
- On the right is the Korean flag, to represent the heritage of our martial art.
- In the center is the Moo Duk Kwan flag, Kwan Gi, which symbolizes the goals and ideals central to our training.

The Moo Duk Kwan Flag (Kwan Gi)

The Moo Duk Kwan® flag (Kwan Gi) represents the organization and Soo Bahk Do® the martial art. It has both physical and philosophical significance in our training.

1. **Gold Fist:** The Moo Duk Kwan® fist stands for justice, for honor, and for unity bearing strength.

2. **Green Leaves:** The 14 leaves on each side of the wreath represent peace and the 14 provinces of Korea.

3. **Red Berries:** The berries represent the fruitful results of training and the six major continents. Red comes from the "Yang".

4. **Blue Scroll:** The blue scroll at the bottom of the flag represents knowledge. In the Founder's words, "the martial artist should also be a scholar." The color blue comes from the Um.

5. **SOO** (*character on the bottom left*): Meaning "hand". It is also "Soo" from Soo Bahk Do® to indicate its influence.

6. **MOO** (*character in the middle*): Meaning martial or military. It is a composite of "stop" and "sword" or "fighting". This symbol represents the idea that the central purpose of Soo Bahk Do® training is to be able to avoid conflict and stop fighting between people and to resolve conflicts within ourselves.

7. **BAHK** (*character on the bottom right*): Meaning to "strike"

American Flag

The seven red stripes stand for courage. The six white stripes stand for purity of nation. The 13 stripes in total stand for the thirteen original colonies. The fifty stars stand for the fifty states of the United States of America. The color blue on the Flag stands for justice.

South Korean Flag (Taegukgi)

The white represents the land (peace and purity). The circle (Taeguk) represents the people. The red is the "Yang" (active) and the blue is the "Um" (passive). The middle line between the Um and Yang is the Il Hwan, which represents opposites, continuous motion, divided equally and perfectly balanced. The Trigrams represent movement and harmony as fundamental principles.

The Meaning of the Trigrams are as follows:

Trigram	Korean Name	Element	Season	Direction	Virtue
☰	Geon	Heaven	Spring	East	Humanity
☲	Ri	Fire	Autumn	South	Justice
☵	Gam	Water	Winter	North	Intelligence
☷	Gon	Earth	Summer	West	Courtesy

Courtesy and Etiquette

Moo Duk Kwan® schools teach the traditional Korean martial art of Soo Bahk Do® based on respect for all life. It is important to develop this respect of our art, our country, our Grandmaster, Senior Dan members, and all members in accordance with Moo Duk Kwan® principles and philosophy.

General Situations in the Do Jang:

- **Entering and leaving a Do Jang:** Upon entering a Do Jang, pause by the entrance, face the flags, and salute by holding the right hand open and across the chest with palm facing the heart and bow in the direction of the senior member within the Do Jang. This demonstrates respect and appreciation for our country and our art. You should perform this discipline upon entering and leaving the Do Jang.

- **Preparing to train:** Upon entering the Do Jang, you must show respect by personal preparation. Cease talking and try to quiet yourself both mentally and physically. Turn your thoughts towards your training. These personal actions help you to create an inner atmosphere of "Jong Sook," quiet internal peace.

- **Recognizing senior members:** As you first enter the Do Jang, it is appropriate to recognize each senior member with a bow. The bow is performed by standing at attention and bowing from the waist about 45 degrees. The senior member will bow in return. While in the Do Jang, if a senior member enters, you should recognize him/ her with a bow from the attention position. Junior members should always bow to senior members first. The senior member, in return, bows back.

- **Recognizing Sa Bom Nim or Chief Instructor:** Upon the entrance of the Sa Bom Nim or the chief instructor, the most senior member of the class will call the class to attention "Cha Ryut" and command "Kyung Ret." The class will then recognize the Sa Bom Nim or the chief instructor with a bow.

- **Joining a class in progress or late entrance:** When you arrive after a class is in session you should enter the Do Jang quietly and stand at the door. First, bow in the direction of the flags. Then remain at an attention position by the door until you are recognized by the instructor. After being recognized by the instructor, bow to the instructor and walk behind the other members of the class to assume your appropriate position with the class.

- **Receiving Instruction:** At any time, before, after, or during class, when the instructor or any senior member offers personal correction of instruction to a junior member, the junior member must stand at attention (if possible). At the completion of the instruction, the junior member must bow and repeat "Thank you, Sir/Ma'am." This shows appreciation and respect. A junior member should refrain from correcting a senior member in the Do Jang.

- **Closing ceremonies:** At the end of the class, after the closing ceremonies, all class members should bow to their instructor.

- **How to ask a question:** During the class when you have a question, raise your hand. When the instructor recognizes you, stand at attention, bow, and then ask your question. After the answer has been received, you should bow and then say, "Thank you, Sir/Ma'am."

- **How to be excused:** During the class when you need to be excused (to go to the restroom or due to illness), you should raise your hand to gain recognition from the instructor. After getting permission from the instructor, bow and act accordingly. When you are able to rejoin the class, stand at attention on the outskirts of the room until recognized by the instructor. Once recognized by the instructor, you may bow and rejoin the class.

- **How to end class:** When a junior ends class, he/she should pay respect to the highest ranking senior member. In situations where there is more than one senior member, the class should bow to the highest ranking member only.

Entering an Instructor's Office

1. Never walk into your instructor's office unannounced. Always knock first at the door and wait for instructions.

2. Upon seeing the instructor, the student bows from the attention position.

3. The student stands until recognized by the instructor (if asked to be seated, student may sit), then the student begins the conversation.

4. The student remains standing at attention during the conversation unless otherwise instructed by the instructor.

5. It is the instructor's responsibility to show respect to his/her student by extending the courtesy to him/her to be seated before the conversation begins.

6. When the conversation is concluded, the student thanks the instructor and walks backward (not showing his/her back to the instructor) until he/she reaches the door. The student bows before exiting.
   Note:
   - *Students should not sit at the instructor's desk at any time, whether in the presence or absence of the instructor.*
   - *The conversation between the instructor and the student should always maintain a tone of respect and the words "Sir" or "Ma'am" should be used, regardless if you are in or out of your Do Bok.*

Communication by Letter
NOTE: *The proper courtesy and etiquette explained below also applies to texting, emailing and social media posts.*

- **How to address the letter:** When writing letters, always include the title of the person whether he or she is your senior or junior. If the person has no title, use the title Mr./Mrs./Miss/or Ms. *(Note: Use of Korean titles follow the person's name).*
  - Seniors writing to junior: Do not include the "Nim"
    - Example: John Doe Kyo Sa
  - Juniors writing to senior: Include the "Nim"
    - Example: John Doe Sa Bom Nim
- **How to start the letter:**
  - Seniors writing to juniors: Do not use "Nim".
    - Include the official title with the proper name.
    - Example: Dear John Doe Kyo Sa
  - If the relationship warrants, seniors may also use the first name.
    - Example: Dear John Doe
  - The proper name with no title except Mr./Mrs./Miss/or Ms.
    - Example: Dear Mr. Doe
  - Juniors writing to seniors: Always use the official title (including "Nim") and the proper name

- **How to close or sign the letter:**
    - Seniors writing to juniors: Never use your title (Master, Mr., Mrs., Sa Bom, or Kyo Sa) in front of the name. As a courtesy, you may give an official title or position such as "Chairman" or school name.
        - Example:
            Sincerely,   Sincerely,
            John Doe   John Doe
            Chairman   Doe's Soo Bahk Do
    - Juniors writing to seniors: When writing to a senior, no matter how high your rank, you sign just your name and not your rank or position. A junior shows disrespect to a senior by signing a letter as "Master John Doe" or "John Doe Kyo Sa". It is better to be humble and not flaunt your title.
        - Example:
            Sincerely,
            John Doe
            Your student

Communication by Phone
- Continuation of class manners and discipline should be extended when talking over the phone to your instructor.
- Student should use "Sir" or "Ma'am" during the phone conversation.

At a Social Event (Restaurant)
1. The student should be in the restaurant earlier than the expected arrival of the instructor.
2. When the instructor arrives, all students should rise and greet the instructor with a bow.
3. The instructor should be seated first and the students should begin to be seated generally rotating from the left side of the instructor to the right according to seniority. Seniors sit down first and others follow. If already seated, the student should rise and remain standing until all his/her seniors are seated.
4. Placement of seating is flexible. However, it is usual for the seniors to be placed next to the instructor. (This is not a rigid rule).
5. When the food is served, the student should wait until the instructor starts to eat first and then the student may begin.
    Note:
    - *Students should not smoke or drink alcohol while the instructor is present, unless the instructor gives prior permission.*
    - *If a student has the opportunity to be in the presence of the Grandmaster, proper attire must be worn (Suit and tie for men. Dress, suit, or appropriate pant outfit for women).*

Korean Terminology

COURTESY AND ETIQUETTE
Hello .... An'nyong Ha Sip Ni Ka
Thank You .... Kahm Sa Ham Ni Da
You're Welcome .... Chun Mhan Eh Yo
Go in peace (Good Bye) .... An'nyong Hi Ka Sip Sio
Stay in peace (Guest would say as they leave) ..... An'nyong Hi Key Sip Sio

GENERAL TERMINOLOGY
Name of the art we study .... Soo Bahk Do®
Hand .... Soo
Strike .... Bahk
Way .... Do
Name of the Organization or style .... Moo Duk Kwan®
Martial (Prevent Conflict) .... Moo
Virtue .... Duk
School .... Kwan
Term of respect .... Nim
(Similar to 'Sir,' 'Ma'am,' or 'Honorable')
Grandmaster, head of Moo Duk Kwan® .... Kwan Jang Nim
Certified Instructor (4th Dan and up) .... Sa Bom Nim
(Reserved for Certified Instructors)
Certified Instructor (2nd Dan and higher) .... Kyo Sa Nim
(Reserved for Certified Instructors)
Senior member .... Sun Beh Nim
Junior member .... Hu Beh
Degree .... Dan
(Holder of midnight blue belt)
Grade .... Gup
(Holder of color belt under midnight blue)
Senior Dan holder (4th Dan and up) .... Ko Dan Ja
Dan holder (1st Dan through 3rd Dan) .... Yu Dan Ja
Dan number .... Dan Bon
Gup holder .... Yu Gup Ja
Student member .... Kwan Won
Beginner .... Cho Bo Ja
Training hall (school) .... Do Jang
Training suit (uniform) .... Do Bok
Belt .... Dee
National flag .... Kuk Gi

Flag of a style or school of Soo Bahk Do® .... Kwan Gi
(Such as Moo Duk Kwan® Gi)
Basic .... Gi Cho
Basic Movements .... Gi Cho Bup
Form .... Hyung
Sparring .... Dae Ryun
Self-defense .... Ho Sin Sul

Hand techniques .... Soo Gi
Foot techniques .... Jok Gi

Block .... Mahk Kee
Attack .... Kong Kyuk
Kick .... Cha Gi

Low Part .... Ha Dan
Middle Part .... Choong Dan
High Part .... Sang Dan

Front .... Ahp
Side .... Yup
Back .... Dwi

Right Side .... O Rin Jok
Left Side .... Wen Jok

Yell .... Ki Hap
Balance .... Choong Shim

Focus of eyes or direction of line of sight .... Shi Sun
Internal power or control in exercise .... Neh Gung
External power or control in exercise .... Weh Gung
Mental power or control in exercise .... Shim Gung

Balance .... Pyung
Security, Confidence .... Ahn
Seven .... Chil
Star .... Sung
Moo Do Jaseh .... Military – Way – Figure (Ja) – Force (Seh)
Note: Incorporating the 5 Moo Do Values in Action – Attitude and Presence.

COMMANDS IN TRAINING

Attention	Cha Ryut
Bow	Kyung Ret
	(*Ret* is pronounced "Nyeh")
Ready	Jhoon Bee
Begin	Si Jak
Return	Ba Ro
Relax (rest)	Shio
Uniform Neaten / Tidy	Do Bok Dan Jung
5 Minute Break	O Bon Hyusik
Sit (please)	An Jo Sip Shio or An Jo Seh Oh
Turn	Tora
Turn to rear	Dwi Ro Tora
Ready for kicking	Bal Cha Gi Jhoon Bee
Count	Ku Ryung
By the count	Ku Ryung Eh Mat Cho So
Without count	Ku Ryung Up Shi
Intermediate position	Choong Gan Jaseh
Again or repeat	Dasi
Movement	Dong Jak
Forward movement	Chun Jin
Sideways movement	Wheng Jin
	(*Wheng* is pronounced "Hweng")
Backward movement	Hu Jin
Movement with opposite hand and foot forward	Yuk Jin
Move to this location (i.e. *Ho Sin Sul, Wee Chi Ro*)	Wee Chi Ro
Return to your last position (previous location)	Chun Wee Chi
Return to your original location	Won Wee Chi

COMMANDS IN STARTING AND ENDING CLASS

Attention	Cha Ryut
Salute to flag	Kuk Gi Bay Ray
Return	Ba Ro
Sit	An Jo
Meditation	Muk Nyum
Return	Ba Ro
Bow to certified Master instructor	Sa Bom Nim Keh Kyung Ret
Bow to (certified) instructor	Kyo Sa Nim Keh Kyung Ret
Bow to senior member(s)	Sun Bae Nim Keh Kyung Ret
Bow to partner (each other)	Sahng Ho Kan Eh Kyung Ret
Bow to Judge or Examiner	Shim Sa Kwan Nim Keh Kyung Ret
Bow to the Grandmaster	Kwan Jang Nim Keh Kyung Ret
	(*Ret* is pronounced "Nyet")

NUMBERS (BON)

Native Korean System
One	Ha Na
Two	Dool
Three	Set
Four	Net
Five	Da Sot
Six	Yuh Sot
Seven	Il Gop
Eight	Yo Dull
Nine	Ah Hope
Ten	Yohl

Sino-Korean System (Based on Chinese Numbers)
First	Il
Second	E
Third	Sam
Fourth	Sa
Fifth	O
Sixth	Yuk
Seventh	Chil
Eighth	Pal
Ninth	Gu
Tenth	Sip
Twenty	E Sip
Thirty	Sam Sip
Forty	Sa Sip
Fifty	O Sip
Sixty	Yuk Sip
Seventy	Chil Sip
Eighty	Pal Sip
Ninety	Gu Sip
One Hundred	Baek

BASIC STANCES (GI CHO JASEH)
Ready stance	Jhoon Bee Jaseh
Front stance	Chun Gul Jaseh
Back stance	Hu Gul Jaseh
Horse stance	Kee Ma Jaseh
Side stance	Sa Ko Rip Jaseh
Cross-legged stance	Kyo Cha Rip Jaseh

HAND TECHNIQUES (SOO GI)

Defensive
(The addition of the term "Teul Oh" indicates twisting)

A) Closed fist - Front stance
    Low block, front stance .... Ha Dan Mahk Kee
    High block, front stance .... Sang Dan Mahk Kee
    Inside/outside block .... Ahneso Pahkuro Mahk Kee
    Outside/inside block .... Pahkeso Ahnuro Mahk Kee
    Two fist middle block .... Chun Gul Ssang Soo
        Ahneso Pahkuro Mahk Kee
    Two fist low block (X block) .... Ssang Soo Ha Dan Mahk Kee

B) Closed fist - Back stance
    Low block .... Hu Gul Ha Dan Mahk Kee
    High block .... Hu Gul Sang Dan Mahk Kee
    Middle block .... Hu Gul Ahneso Pahkuro Mahk Kee
    Outside/inside block (wrist)........ Hu Gul Pahkeso Ahnuro Mahk Kee
    Two fist middle block .... Hu Gul Ssang Soo
        Ahneso Pahkuro Mahk Kee
    Two fist low block .... Hu Gul Ssang Soo Ha Dan Mahk Kee

C) Open hand - Front stance
    Two hand high block (X block) .... Ssang Soo Sang Dan Mahk Kee

D) Open hand - Back stance
    Outside/inside block, heel of palm .... Hu Gul Jang Kwon
        Pahkeso Ahnuro Mahk Kee
    Ground block with knife hand .... Choi Ha Dan Soo Do Mahk Kee
    Low knife hand block .... Hu Gul Ha Dan Soo Do Mahk Kee
    High knife hand block .... Hu Gul Sang Dan Soo Do Mahk Kee
    Middle knife hand block .... Hu Gul Choong Dan
        Soo Do Mahk Kee

E) Open hand - Cross-legged stance
    Foot Holding defense .... Bal Ja Ba Mahk Kee
       (Palm heels together)

Offensive
(The addition of the term "Teul Oh" indicates twisting)

A) Closed fist - Forward stance
    Middle punch .... Choong Dan Kong Kyuk
    High punch .... Sang Dan Kong Kyuk

B) Closed fist - Horse stance
    Side punch .... Wheng Jin Kong Kyuk

C) Closed fist - Back stance
    Reverse punch .... Yuk Jin Kong Kyuk

D) Fist, Horse Stance
    Punching Exercise .... Pal Put Ki

E) Open hand - Front stance
    Spear hand attack .... Kwan Soo Kong Kyuk
    Knife hand attack .... Soo Do Kong Kyuk
    Reverse knife hand attack .... Yuk Soo Do Kong Kyuk

F) Open hand, Back stance
    Knife hand attack .... Hu Gul Soo Do Kong Kyuk

G) Other hand techniques
    Plier hand, web of thumb .... Jip Kye Son
    Palm heel .... Jang Kwon
    Upper wrist .... Sohn Mok Deung
    Inner or outer side of wrist .... Pal Mok

Other Hand Attacks (Kong Kyuk)
    Forefist .... Chung Kwon
    Backfist .... Kap Kwon
    Knuckle spear hand .... Ban Jul Kwan Soo
        (All four second knuckles)
    Soft fist .... Yoo Kwon
        (Using second knuckles of first and second fingers)
    Hammer fist .... Kwon Do
    One finger spear hand .... Il Ji Kwan Soo
    Two finger spear hand .... E Ji Kwan Soo
    One finger fist .... Il Ji Kwon
        (Using middle knuckle or forefinger knuckle)

Elbow attack
(The addition of the term "Teul Oh" indicates twisting)

    Front stance, elbow attack .... Chun Gul Jaseh
                                                    Pahl Koop Kong Kyuk
    Side stance, elbow attack .... Sa Ko Rip Jaseh
                                                    Pahl Koop Kong Kyuk

FOOT TECHNIQUES (JOK GI)
Offensive
(The addition of the term "E Dan" indicates jumping kick. The addition of the term "podo" means to thrust)

Front thrust kick	Ahp Cha Nut Gi
Front side kick	Yup Cha Gi
Front stretch kick	Ahp Podo Oll Ri Gi
Side stretch kick	Yup Podo Oll Ri Gi
Side thrust kick	Yup Podo Cha Gi
Roundhouse kick	Dollyo Cha Gi
Back kick	Dwi Cha Gi
Spinning back thrust kick	Dwi Podo Cha Gi
Inside/outside kick	Ahneso Pahkuro Cha Gi
Outside/inside kick	Pahkeso Ahnuro Cha Gi
Spinning inside to outside kick	Dwi Ahneso Pahkuro Cha Gi
Side hook kick	Yup Hu Ri Gi
Long back spinning hook kick	Dwi Hu Ri Gi
Knee kick	Moo Roop Cha Gi
Stomping kick	Chit Pahl Gi
Front pushing kick	Ahp Mee Ro Cha Gi
Reverse roundhouse kick	Peet Cha Gi
Double kick, in sequence	Du Bon Cha Gi
Double kick, same time	Ssang Bal Cha Gi
Continual or combination kicking	Yeon Sok Cha Gi

Defensive

Outside/inside foot block	Pahkeso Ahnuro Bal Cha Mahk Kee
Inside/outside foot block	Ahneso Pahkuro Bal Cha Mahk Kee

Areas of the Foot

Bottom of the foot	Bal Ba Dak Mit
Outer edge of the foot	Bal Yup Koom Chi
Ball of the foot	Bal Ahp Koom Chi
Instep	Bal Deung
Heel	Bal Dwi Koom Chi

Commands for Kicking Exercises

Up	Wee Lo
Front (Push Forward)	Ahp Euro
Back	Dwi Lo
Down	A Leh Lo

SPARRING (DAE RYUN)

Three-step sparring..................................Sam Soo Sik Dae Ryun
One-step sparring ....Il Soo Sik Dae Ryun
Free sparring..Ja Yu Dae Ryun
Sparring in a sitting position ....Jua Dae Ryun
Sparring in a lying down position................ Wa Dae Ryun
Stick sparring ....Bong Dae Ryun
Sparring against two or more ....Da Soo In Dae Ryun
Change positions...Kyo Deh
    (Assume partner's position)
Special sparring.. Took Soo Dae Ryun
Short knife sparring .... Dan Do Dae Ryun
Non-contact sparring..Gun Nun Dae Ryun

ANATOMY

Fist ....Chu Mok
Neck .... Mok
Waist ....Hu Ri
Leg..Da Ri
Elbow .... Pal Koop
Knee .... Moo Roop
Chin ....Tuck
Forehead.. Eema
Groin .... Ko Whan
Abdomen .... Dan Jun
Arm .... Pahl
Between mouth and nose (Philtrum) ....In Choong
Hand .... Soo (Sino-Korean)
                                           Sohn (Korean)
Foot..Jok (Sino-Korean)
                                            Bal (Korean)

TOURNAMENT TERMINOLOGY

Start of the match (begin) .... Si Jak
Temporary stop .... Gu Man
Resume match .... Kay Sok
When the match has been stopped without the proclamation of the referee

Time .... Shi Gan
One point .... Han Jom
Two points .... Du Jom
Three points .... Seh Jom
No point .... Moo Jom
Loser .... Pae Ja
Winner .... Soong Ja
A draw .... Bee Gim
Foul .... Ban Chik
Warning .... Kyong Go
Holding .... Boot Jap Um
Judgment .... Shim Sa
The end of the match .... E Sang
Victory of the white .... Beck Soong
Victory of the red .... Hong Soong
Extending the time of the match .... Yon Jang Jon
Disqualified .... Ja Kyok Sang Shil
Ordering the contestants
    in to the match area .... Sun Soo Eep Jang
Ordering the contestants
    to their fixed positions .... Sun Soo Wi Chi Jung Nee

OTHER

Standardization .... Il Kwan Seong
Connection .... Iyeon Kwan Seong
Strengthen Identity .... Shin Boon Khang Hwa
High Level of Technique .... Ko Cha Won Ki Sul
ONE Moo Duk Kwan .... Hana Eui Moo Duk Kwan
Line – Speed – Beauty .... Seon Sok Mi
Earth Energy .... Ji Gi
Heaven Energy .... Tcheon Gi
Sincere Effort .... No Ryok
Intent .... Eui Do
Mind .... Ma Um
Heaviness (as in presence-attitude / Moo Do Jaseh) .... Moo Geh

MOO DUK KWAN® RANK PROGRESSION FOR SOO BAHK DO®

Current Rank	Minimum Training by Months / Years for Next Rank Test	Minimum Training by Hours / Class for Next Rank Test	Minimum Federation Membership Time Requirement	Rank Testing For
Tiger Tot	See Tiger Tot Training Guidelines	Varies	Memberships available, but not required	Tiger Tot
10th Gup	1 month	8 hours	New Member	9th Gup
9th Gup	2 months	16 hours	2 months	8th Gup
8th Gup	2-3 months	16-24 hours	7 months	7th Gup
7th Gup	2-3 months	16-24 hours	9 months	6th Gup
6th Gup	2-3 months	16-24 hours	11 months	5th Gup
5th Gup	3-4 months	24-32 hours	14 months	4th Gup
4th Gup	3-4 months	24-32 hours	17 months	3rd Gup
3rd Gup	3-4 months	24-32 hours	20 months	2nd Gup
2nd Gup	6 months	48 hours	26 months	1st Gup
1st Gup	6 months	48 hours	33 months	1st Dan
1st Dan	2 years	-	5 years	2nd Dan
2nd Dan	3 years	-	8 years	3rd Dan
3rd Dan	4 years	-	12 years	4th Dan
4th Dan	5 years	-	17 years	5th Dan
5th Dan	6 years	-	23 years	6th Dan
6th Dan	7 years	-	30 years	7th Dan
7th Dan	8 years	-	38 years	8th Dan
8th Dan	9 years	-	47 years	9th Dan

NOTE: THE MINIMUM TRAINING TIME MUST BE CONSECUTIVE MONTHS OR YEARS.

General Information for Test Candidates

A student's eligibility to test for rank promotion and instructor certification is at the discretion of the student's personal certified instructor. The U.S. Federation only recognizes Gup rank and Jo Kyo recommendations received from certified instructors operating certified schools. Regional Examiners, the TAC, and other federation officials will review and confirm a certified instructor's recommendation for a student who intends to test for Dan or Ko Dan Ja rank plus Kyo Bom and Kyo Sa or Sa Bom instructor certification.

Test Eligibility

A certified instructor evaluates many aspects of a student's training for consideration of rank promotion or instructor certification. For example, overall performance, attendance, behavior, maturity and leadership characteristics. Students must be Federation members in good standing and membership time must equals or exceed training time.

Prior to recommending a student for rank promotion or instructor certification, the instructor will determine if the student meets or exceeds:
- Minimum training time requirement
- Minimum age requirement, if specified
- Instructor Certification Applicants Age 18 up
    - Has active Background Check & Continuing Education subscription on Soo Bahk Do Institute
    - Successful Background Check
    - Completed Safety Training
- Instructor's expectations
- TAC technical performance expectations
- TAC academic performance expectations
- Kwan Jang Nim's Vision Participation expectations

Ages for Testing Requirements

The children's requirements are for all practitioners age fourteen (14) and under. Adult requirements are for all practitioners age fifteen (15) and over. Note: At the instructor's discretion additional techniques and information may be taught to children but are not required to pass an exam.

Dan and Ko Dan Ja Eligibility Considerations

Considerations for Dan and Ko Dan Ja candidates include satisfactory and/or exemplary:
- Support of Mission 2000 Objectives
- Support to Vision Objectives (being a certified instructor, school owner, etc.)
- Embodiment of Moo Do Values in all dimensions of life (essays, news coverage, publications, etc.)
- Record of international event participation
- Record of national event participation
- Record of regional event participation
- Record of service and support to the World Moo Duk Kwan
    - Example: Photography, editing, donations, technical services, etc.
- Record of service and support to the national federation
    - Example: Photography, editing, donations, technical services, etc.
- Record of submissions of proposed creative contributions to the art
    - Example: Publications, articles, audio, videos, books
- Certified Instructors: Active Background Check & Continuing Education subscription on Soo Bahk Do® Institute

TIGER TOTS ACHIEVEMENT & BELT RANKING SYSTEM

Objective: The United States Soo Bahk Do Moo Duk Kwan Federation® offers a special ranking system suited for children ages 4-7 years old. The Tiger Tots program provides a special variable term Federation membership opportunity that lasts until age 7 or when the student applies for 8th Gup rank certification.

Minimum allowable timeframe from the start of the Tiger Tot program to 8th Gup rank certification is <u>6 months</u>. Instructor's may use their discretion to define a suitable timeframe between Tiger Tot rank promotions, but the minimum total time cannot be less than 6 months.

Considerations:
- Encourage student growth and personal development through activities that adhere to Moo Duk Kwan principles in their Soo Bahk Do training.
- Facilitate the child's inclusion in a regular Soo Bahk Do training program upon completion of the Tiger Tot program.
- Develop character by increasing the child's self-esteem in a positive learning environment emphasizing Moo Duk Kwan philosophy.
- It is recommended that some basic safety rules be included into the program.
- Provide flexibility in the requirements concerning achievements within the Tiger Tot program.

Teaching Aids and Activities:
Considering the very short attention span of small children, it is important to have continuous activities that relate to the curriculum. These are some teaching aids and activities that may be considered:
- "Sa Bom or Kyo Sa Nim says" (similar to "Simon Says" game) to improve the child's concentration, basic hand/kicking techniques and terminology.
- Create obstacle courses using varied equipment to develop agility and coordination.
- Use pads for practicing kicking, punching, and blocking.
- Coloring books and work books with connect the dot/word games.
- The Eight Key Concepts taught in Moo Duk Kwan schools are an excellent aid to help young children in their development to be future Soo Bahk Do practitioners as well as respected citizens in our society.

Special Notes:
- Utilizing too many games and prizes as a tool for children's motivation can be unhealthy in Soo Bahk Do® practice.
- During the process of achieving Tiger Tot's belt stripes, it is very important for instructors to congratulate children for their achievement in discipline, rather than the belt stripe itself.
- An instructor's high energy and enjoyment while teaching children will positively influence a child's motivation to learn Soo Bahk Do®.

Conclusion:

In conclusion, the Tiger Tot Program should facilitate a smooth transition for children ages four through seven into the Moo Duk Kwan® without losing quality at an early age. This program emphasizes preparing the "Tiger Tot" for future Soo Bahk Do® training. This is accomplished by developing their character and self-esteem in a positive learning environment by using specific teaching methodologies.

Tiger Tots Belt Ranking System

The following are the eight levels for a child's achievements in the Tiger Tot program, from age four to seven. Once all levels have been achieved, it is recommended that the instructor guide the student into a regular children's program by testing for 8th Gup.

It is suggested that the requirements be taught in a creative fashion with good sense of humor that addresses the aptitudes and learning abilities of the children.

The recommended number of classes and duration is twice per week, 30 to 45 minutes per class. We recommend a minimum of six weeks between evaluating their achievements.

Join the Federation and become a registered member

Patches

1st Rank *(Orange Stripe)*

2nd Rank *(2nd Orange Stripe)*

3rd Rank *(Green Stripe)*

4th Rank *(2nd Green Stripe)*

5th Rank *(Red Stripe)*

6th Rank *(2nd Red Stripe)*

7th Rank *(Blue Stripe)*

8th Rank *(2nd Blue Stripe)*

8th Gup *(Orange Belt)*

Moo Duk Kwan® Technical Curriculum For Soo Bahk Do®

Effective January 1, 2018 the following testing requirements represent the minimum proficiency to advance in rank within the United States Soo Bahk Do Moo Duk Kwan Federation®.

INSTRUCTOR NOTE: *Minimum Requirements listed. Instructor's may use their discretion to add or adjust content depending on the student's age and abilities.*

10ᵀᴴ GUP TO 9ᵀᴴ GUP | PROMOTION REQUIREMENTS |

General Requirements
The following are minimum requirements to be eligible for promotion:
- Age requirements: No minimum age
- Proof of current Federation membership (Federation ID Card)
- Membership time must equal or exceed required training time
- Must be of sound moral character

Expectations of Performance
Candidate should be able to demonstrate the following:
- Proper stance and Shi Sun
- Proper placement of elbows in intermediate and completion position for hand techniques
- Proper placement of knee in chamber position for kicking techniques
- Proper striking of the weapon in hand and foot techniques
- Proper protocol within the school (Do Jang)

Culture, Terminology, and History
Candidate should be able to explain his or her understanding of the following:
- Name of the art you study: Soo Bahk Do
- Name of the style: Moo Duk Kwan
- Name of the Founder and current President of Moo Duk Kwan®
- Uniform: Do Bok
- School: Do Jang
- Protocol for entering and leaving the Do Jang

10ᵀᴴ GUP TO 9ᵀᴴ GUP | DEMONSTRATION OF ABILITY |

HAND TECHNIQUES	SOO GI
Low Block	Ha Dan Mahk Kee
High Block	Sang Dan Mahk Kee
Middle Punch	Choong Dan Kong Kyuk
High Punch	Sang Dan Kong Kyuk

FOOT TECHNIQUES	JOK GI
Front Thrust Kick	Ahp Cha Nut Gi

FORMS	HYUNG
Basic Form # 1 *(Optional)*	Gi Cho Hyung Il Bu

ONE-STEP SPARRING	IL SOO SIK
Optional	

SELF-DEFENSE	HO SIN SUL
Optional	

FREE SPARRING	JA YU DAE RYUN
Optional	

BREAKING	KYOK PA
Not Required	

Optional Study Resource:
Soo Bahk Do® Institute Video Subscription **For Your Target Rank**

9ᵀᴴ Gup to 8ᵀᴴ Gup | Promotion Requirements |

General Requirements
The following are minimum requirements to be eligible for promotion:
- Age requirements: No minimum age
- Proof of current federation membership (Federation ID Card)
- Membership time must equal or exceed required training time
- Must be of sound moral character

Expectations of Performance
Candidate should be able to demonstrate the following:
- Proper stance and Shi Sun
- Proper placement of elbows in intermediate and completion position for hand techniques
- Proper placement of knee in chamber position for kicking techniques
- Proper striking of the weapon in hand and foot techniques
- Proper protocol within the school (Do Jang)

Culture, Terminology, and History
Candidate should be able to explain his or her understanding of the following:
- What is your favorite 8 Key Concept and how does it help you in your daily life (school, work, spirit, etc.)?
- 8 Key Concepts
- Instructor: Sa Bom Nim / Kyo Sa Nim / Jo Kyo Nim
- Courage: Yong Gi
- Seniors / Juniors: Sun Beh / Huh Beh

9ᵗʰ Gup to 8ᵗʰ Gup | Demonstration of Ability |

HAND TECHNIQUES	SOO GI
High Block	Sang Dan Mahk Kee
Inside to Outside Block	Ahneso Pakuro Mahk Kee

FOOT TECHNIQUES	JOK GI
Roundhouse Kick	Dollyo Cha Gi
Inside to Outside Kick	Ahneso Pakuro Cha Gi

FORMS	HYUNG
Basic Form # 1	Gi Cho Hyung Il Bu
Basic Form # 2	Gi Cho Hyung E Bu

ONE-STEP SPARRING   **IL SOO SIK**
Extra Credit *(Content At Instructor's Discretion)*

SELF-DEFENSE   **HO SIN SUL**
Extra Credit *(Content At Instructor's Discretion)*

FREE SPARRING   **JA YU DAE RYUN**
Extra Credit *(Content At Instructor's Discretion)*

BREAKING   **KYOK PA**
Not Required

Optional Study Resource:
Soo Bahk Do® Institute Video Subscription For Your Target Rank

8ᵀᴴ Gup to 7ᵀᴴ Gup | Promotion Requirements |

General Requirements
The following are minimum requirements to be eligible for promotion:
- Age requirements: No minimum age
- Proof of current federation membership (Federation ID Card)
- Membership time must equal or exceed required training time
- Must be of sound moral character

Expectations of Performance
Candidate should be able to demonstrate the following:
- Proper stance and Shi Sun
- Proper placement of elbows in intermediate and completion position for hand techniques
- Proper placement of knee in chamber position for kicking techniques
- Proper striking of the weapon in hand and foot techniques
- Proper protocol within the school (Do Jang)

Culture, Terminology, and History
Candidate should be able to explain his or her understanding of the following:
- Concentration: Chung Shin Tong Il
- Discuss the benefits of the 8 Key Concepts in your daily life (activities)
- Count from 1 to 10 in Korean

8ᵗʰ Gup to 7ᵗʰ Gup | Demonstration of Ability |

HAND TECHNIQUES	SOO GI
Outside Inside Block	Pahkeso Ahnuro Mahk Kee
Side Punch	Wheng Jin Kong Kyuk
Elbow Attack	Pahl Koop Kong Kyuk
Back Stance, Side Inside to Outside Block	Hu Gul Yup Mahk Kee

FOOT TECHNIQUES	JOK GI
Front Stretch Kick	Ahp Podo Oll Ri Gi
Side Thrust Kick	Yup Podo Cha Gi
Jump Front Thrust Kick	E Dan Ahp Cha Nut Gi

FORMS	HYUNG
Basic Form # 2	Gi Cho Hyung E Bu
Basic Form # 3	Gi Cho Hyung Sam Bu

ONE-STEP SPARRING	IL SOO SIK
Extra Credit *(Content At Instructor's Discretion)*	

SELF-DEFENSE	HO SIN SUL
Extra Credit *(Content At Instructor's Discretion)*	

FREE SPARRING	JA YU DAE RYUN
Extra Credit *(Content At Instructor's Discretion)*	
Demonstrate any two White Belt Sparring Combinations *(Optional)*	

BREAKING	KYOK PA
Adults *(15 +)*	Pahl Koop Kong Kyuk or Ahp Cha Nut Gi
Children *(Under 15 Years of Age)*	None

Optional Study Resource:
Soo Bahk Do® Institute Video Subscription For Your Target Rank

7ᵀᴴ Gup to 6ᵀᴴ Gup | Promotion Requirements |

General Requirements
The following are minimum requirements to be eligible for promotion:
- Age requirements: No minimum age
- Proof of current federation membership (Federation ID Card)
- Membership time must equal or exceed required training time
- Must be of sound moral character

Expectations of Performance
Candidate should be able to demonstrate the following:
- Proper Ki Hap, spirit, Shi Sun, and Moo Do Jaseh
- Proper focus of weapon to target
- Proper respect to senior and junior members
- Proper weapon discipline
- Proper process of 'chain of command' in hand/foot basics
- Proper demonstration of speed control (Wan Gup)

Culture, Terminology, and History
Candidate should be able to explain his or her understanding of the following:
- Discuss any resulted experience outside the Do Jang connected to the 8 Key Concepts
- Belt colors and meaning
- *Terminology:*

ENGLISH	KOREAN
Basic	Gi Cho
Attack	Kong Kyuk
Defense	Mahk Kee
Bow	Kyung Ret
Form	Hyung
Meditation	Muk Nyum
Begin	Si Jak
Sparring	Dae Ryun
Attention	Cha Ryut
Return	Ba Ro
Endurance	In Neh

7ᵀᴴ Gup to 6ᵀᴴ Gup | Demonstration of Ability |

HAND TECHNIQUES	SOO GI
Low Knife Hand Block	Ha Dan Soo Do Mahk Kee
Two Fist Middle Block in a Front Stance	Chun Gul Ssang Soo Ahneso Pahkuro Mahk Kee
Two Fist Middle Block in a Back Stance	Hu Gul Ssang Soo Ahneso Pahkuro Mahk Kee
Cross Body Middle Punch	Teul Oh Choong Dan Kong Kyuk
Cross Body High Punch	Teul Oh Sang Dan Kong Kyuk

FOOT TECHNIQUES	JOK GI
Inside To Outside Kick	Ahneso Pahkuro Cha Gi
Spinning Back Thrust Kick	Dwi Podo Cha Gi
Hand and Foot Combinations Using All Known Techniques	

FORMS	HYUNG
Gi Cho Hyung Sam Bu	
Pyung Ahn Cho Dan	

ONE-STEP SPARRING	IL SOO SIK
Adults	1 - 2
Children	1

SELF-DEFENSE	HO SIN SUL
Adults	Cross Hand Wrist Grips (1-2)
Children	Cross Hand Wrist Grips (1)

FREE SPARRING	JA YU DAE RYUN
Free Sparring	
Extra Credit - *Demonstrate any two Orange Belt Sparring Combinations*	

BREAKING	KYOK PA
Adults *(15 +)*	Pahl Koop Kong Kyuk or Yup Podo Cha Gi
Children *(Under 15 Years of Age)*	None

Optional Study Resource:
Soo Bahk Do® Institute Video Subscription For Your Target Rank

6ᵗʰ Gᴜᴘ ᴛᴏ 5ᵗʰ Gᴜᴘ | Pʀᴏᴍᴏᴛɪᴏɴ Rᴇǫᴜɪʀᴇᴍᴇɴᴛs |

General Requirements
The following are minimum requirements to be eligible for promotion:
- Age requirements: No minimum age
- Proof of current federation membership (Federation ID Card)
- Membership time must equal or exceed required training time
- Must be of sound moral character

Expectations of Performance
A candidate should be able to demonstrate the following:
- Proper Ki Hap, spirit, and Moo Do Jaseh
- Proper focus (Shi Sun)
- Proper respect to senior and junior members
- Proper weapon discipline
- Proper process of 'chain of command' in hand/foot basics
- Proper demonstration of speed control (Wan Gup)

Culture, Terminology, and History
Candidate should be able to explain his or her understanding of the following:
- Adults: Discuss personal benefits from your Soo Bahk Do training and the 8 Key Concepts.
- Children: List favorite 8 Key Concept and why
- Meaning of Pyung Ahn
- Honesty: Chung Jik
- Sino-Korean (Chinese) Numbers: Il - Ship
- Questions about protocol and etiquette

6ᵀᴴ GUP TO 5ᵀᴴ GUP | DEMONSTRATION OF ABILITY |

HAND TECHNIQUES	SOO GI
Middle Knife Hand Block	Choong Dan Soo Do Mahk Kee
Two Fist Low X Block	Ha Dan Ssang Soo Mahk Kee
Spear Hand Attack	Kwan Soo Kong Kyuk
Hammer Fist	Kwon Do Kong Kyuk

FOOT TECHNIQUES	JOK GI
Outside to Inside Kick	Pahkeso Ahnuro Cha Gi
Jumping Side Kick	E Dan Yup Podo Cha Gi
Hand and Foot Combinations Using All Known Techniques	

FORMS	HYUNG
Pyung Ahn Cho Dan	
Pyung Ahn E Dan	

ONE-STEP SPARRING	IL SOO SIK
Adults	3 - 4
Children	3 *(Side Step with block and counter only)*

SELF-DEFENSE	HO SIN SUL
Adults	Cross Hand Wrist Grips (3-4)
Children	Cross Hand Wrist Grips (2)

FREE SPARRING	JA YU DAE RYUN
Free Sparring	
Extra Credit - *Demonstrate any two Green Belt Sparring Combinations*	

BREAKING	KYOK PA
Kwon Do Kong Kyuk or Dwi Podo Cha Gi	

Optional Study Resource:
Soo Bahk Do® Institute Video Subscription *For Your Target Rank*

5ᵀᴴ Gup to 4ᵀᴴ Gup | Promotion Requirements |

General Requirements
The following are minimum requirements to be eligible for promotion:
- Age requirements: No minimum age
- Proof of current federation membership (Federation ID Card)
- Membership time must equal or exceed required training time
- Must be of sound moral character

Expectations of Performance
- Candidate should be able to demonstrate the following:
- Proper Moo Do Jaseh
- Proper focus of weapon to target
- Proper respect to senior and junior members
- Proper weapon discipline
- Proper process of 'chain of command' in hand/foot basics
- Proper demonstration of 8 Key Concepts

Culture, Terminology, and History
Candidate should be able to explain his or her understanding of the following:
- Specify three (3) of your favorite 8 Key Concepts in Korean and explain how they help you in your training
- Humility: Kyum Son
- Basic Terminology
- Significance of the Moo Duk Kwan flag

5ᵀᴴ GUP TO 4ᵀᴴ GUP | DEMONSTRATION OF ABILITY |

HAND TECHNIQUES	SOO GI
High Knife Hand Block	Sang Dan Soo Do Mahk Kee
High Two Hand X Block	Sang Dan Ssang Soo Mahk Kee

FOOT TECHNIQUES	JOK GI
Side Hook Kick	Yup Hu Ri Gi
Hand and Foot Combinations Using All Known Techniques	

FORMS	HYUNG
Pyung Ahn E Dan	
Pyung Ahn Sam Dan	

ONE-STEP SPARRING	IL SOO SIK
Adults	5 - 6
Children	1

SELF-DEFENSE	HO SIN SUL
Adults	Same Side Wrist Grips (1-4)
Children	Same Side Wrist Grips (1)

FREE SPARRING	JA YU DAE RYUN
Free Sparring	
Extra Credit - *Demonstrate any two Green Belt Sparring Combinations*	

BREAKING	KYOK PA
Jang Kwon Kong Kyuk or Dollyo Cha Gi	

Optional Study Resource:
Soo Bahk Do® Institute Video Subscription For Your Target Rank

4ᵀᴴ Gup to 3ᴿᴰ Gup | Promotion Requirements |

General Requirements
The following are minimum requirements to be eligible for promotion:
- Age requirements: No minimum age
- Proof of current federation membership (Federation ID Card)
- Membership time must equal or exceed required training time
- Must be of sound moral character

Expectations of Performance
Candidate should be able to demonstrate the following:
- Proper Moo Do Jaseh
- Proper Shi Sun
- Demonstrate 8 Key Concepts

Culture, Terminology, and History
Candidate should be able to explain his or her understanding of the following:
- Specify any three (3) of your favorite 8 Key Concepts in Korean
- Discuss the benefits of the 8 Key Concepts
- History of the founding of the Moo Duk Kwan
- Five Moo Do Values
- 10 Articles of Faith on Mental Training

4ᵗʰ Gup to 3ʳᵈ Gup | Demonstration of Ability |

HAND TECHNIQUES	SOO GI
Reverse Hammer Fist	Teul Oh Kwon Do Kong Kyuk

FOOT TECHNIQUES	JOK GI
Spinning Hook Kick	Dwi Hu Ri Gi
Jump Roundhouse Kick	E Dan Dollyo Cha Gi
Jump Inside to Outside Kick	E Dan Ahneso Pahkuro Cha Gi

Hand and Foot Combinations Using All Known Techniques, including jump kicks.

FORMS	HYUNG
Pyung Ahn Sam Dan	
Pyung Ahn Sa Dan	

ONE-STEP SPARRING	IL SOO SIK
Adults	7 - 8
Children	3

SELF-DEFENSE	HO SIN SUL
Adults	Two on One Wrist Grips (1-3)
Children	Same Side Wrist Grips (2)

FREE SPARRING	JA YU DAE RYUN
Free Sparring	

Extra Credit - *Demonstrate any two Red Belt Sparring Combinations*

BREAKING	KYOK PA
Teul Oh Choong Dan Kong Kyuk or E Dan Dollyo Cha Gi	

Optional Study Resource:
Soo Bahk Do® Institute Video Subscription For Your Target Rank

3ʳᴰ Gup to 2ⁿᴰ Gup | Promotion Requirements |

General Requirements
The following are minimum requirements to be eligible for promotion:
- Age requirements: No minimum age
- Proof of current federation membership (Federation ID Card)
- Membership time must equal or exceed required training time
- Must be of sound moral character

Expectations of Performance
Candidate should be able to demonstrate the following:
- Distance control
- Demonstration of proper intent during physical demonstration
- Proper acceleration of movement to maximum force
- Demonstration of proper ceremony during Il Soo Sik and Ho Sin Sul

Culture, Terminology, and History
Candidate should be able to explain his or her understanding of the following:
- Share any good social experience as a result of your Soo Bahk Do training
- Moo Duk Kwan history
- 8 Key Concepts
- Philosophy of the art

3ʳᴰ GUP TO 2ᴺᴰ GUP | DEMONSTRATION OF ABILITY |

HAND TECHNIQUES	SOO GI
Ground Block with Knife Hand	Choi Ha Dan Soo Do Mahk Kee

FOOT TECHNIQUES	JOK GI
Spinning Inside to Outside Kick	Dwi Ahneso Pahkuro Cha Gi
Jump Back Kick	E Dan Dwi Cha Gi
Jump Spinning Hook Kick	E Dan Dwi Hu Ri Gi

Hand and Foot Combinations Using All Known Techniques, including jump kicks.

FORMS	HYUNG
Pyung Ahn Sa Dan	
Pyung Ahn O Dan	

ONE-STEP SPARRING	IL SOO SIK
Adults	9 – 10
Children	5

SELF-DEFENSE	HO SIN SUL
Adults	Two on Two Wrist Grips (1-4)
Children	Two on One Wrist Grips (1)

FREE SPARRING	JA YU DAE RYUN
Free Sparring	

Extra Credit - *Demonstrate any two Red Belt Sparring Combinations*

BREAKING	KYOK PA
Yuk Soo Do Kong Kyuk or Yup Hu Ri Gi	

Optional Study Resource:
Soo Bahk Do® Institute Video Subscription For Your Target Rank

2ⁿᴰ Gup to 1ˢᵀ Gup | Promotion Requirements |

General Requirements
The following are minimum requirements to be eligible for promotion:
- Age requirements: No minimum age
- Proof of current federation membership (Federation ID Card)
- Membership time must equal or exceed required training time
- Must be of sound moral character

Expectations of Performance
Candidate should be able to demonstrate the following:
- Distance control
- Demonstration of proper intent during physical demonstration
- Proper acceleration of movement to maximum force
- Demonstration of proper ceremony during Il Soo Sik and Ho Sin Sul

Culture, Terminology, and History
Candidate should be able to explain his or her understanding of the following:
- Describe some of the unique areas of the Moo Duk Kwan
- Personal growth benefits from Soo Bahk Do training
- Meaning of "Do"

2ᴺᴰ Gup to 1ˢᵀ Gup | Demonstration of Ability |

HAND TECHNIQUES	SOO GI
Double Back Fist Strike	Jang Kap Kwon Kong Kyuk

FOOT TECHNIQUES	JOK GI
Inverted Roundhouse Kick	Peet Cha Gi
Jump Spin Inside to Outside Kick	E Dan Dwi Ahneso Pahkuro Cha Gi
Jump Spin Outside to Inside Kick	E Dan Dwi Pahkeso Ahnuro Cha Gi

Hand and Foot Combinations Using All Known Techniques, including jump kicks. Demonstrate use of HuRi and its flow.

FORMS	HYUNG
Pyung Ahn O Dan	
Passai	
Nai Han Ji Cho Dan	

ONE-STEP SPARRING	IL SOO SIK
Adults	11 - 14
Children	7

SELF-DEFENSE	HO SIN SUL
Adults	Side Grips (1-2) and Rear Grips (1-2)
Children	Two on One Wrist Grips (2)

FREE SPARRING	JA YU DAE RYUN
Free Sparring	

Free Sparring combinations utilizing Teul Oh Jang Kap Kwon Kong Kyuk

BREAKING	KYOK PA
Teul Oh Jang Kap Kwon Kong Kyuk or Dwi Hu Ri Gi	

Optional Study Resource:
Soo Bahk Do® Institute Video Subscription For Your Target Rank

1ˢᵗ Gup to Cho Dan | Promotion Requirements |

General Requirements
The following are minimum requirements to be eligible for promotion:
- Age requirements: No minimum age
- Proof of current federation membership (Federation ID Card)
- Membership time must equal or exceed required training time
- Must be of sound moral character

Expectations of Performance
Candidate should be able to demonstrate the following:
- Distance control
- Demonstration of proper intent during physical demonstration
- Proper acceleration of movement to maximum force
- Demonstration of proper ceremony during Il Soo Sik and Ho Sin Sul

Culture, Terminology, and History
Candidate should be able to explain his or her understanding of the following:
- **Written Essay Requirement # 1**
    - What Soo Bahk Do Moo Duk Kwan means to me.
        - Minimum of 1000 words, typewritten and double spaced.
- **Written Essay Requirement # 2**
    - Cite your personal Vision participation and Vision contributions that you have made during your training career and how they have helped achieve measurable success toward vision objectives.
        - 1 Page maximum typewritten document

    - Effective 2019 WMDK has requested each Country to begin acquiring a signed "Consent To Publish" form from Dan essays authors. Those who grant permission may find their essay published on the web or elsewhere. (Examples) Your Dan Shim Sa application packet may be required to include a signed form denying or granting permission to publish your Dan Shim Sa Essays.

1ST GUP TO CHO DAN | DEMONSTRATION OF ABILITY |

HAND / FOOT TECHNIQUES — SOO GI / JOK GI
All Lower Belt Techniques and Requirements
Hand and Foot combinations using known techniques

FORMS — HYUNG
Passai
Chil Sung E Ro Hyung
Nai Han Ji Cho Dan

ONE-STEP SPARRING — IL SOO SIK

Adults	1 - 18
Children	1 - 9 *(odd numbers only)*

SELF-DEFENSE — HO SIN SUL

Adults	All lower belt requirements (Wrist Grips)
Children	1 - 2 Wrist Grips (Cross Hand, Same Side, Two on One and Two on Two)

FREE SPARRING — JA YU DAE RYUN
Free Sparring

IN NEH — ENDURANCE
Thirty (30) seconds of continuous punching (Kee Mah Jaseh) with focus on power, speed and proper direction of hip for maximum effectiveness of each punch. **Goal:** 120 punches with proper technique and form.

BREAKING — KYOK PA
E Dan Dwi Cha Gi (Jump Back Kick) *or*
Yeon Sok Kyok Pa with one Soo Gi and one Jok Gi technique.
NOTE: If the candidate cannot physically perform E Dan Dwi Cha Gi, the Regional Examiner should be consulted prior to testing to define an acceptable break for completion of this requirement.

Optional Study Resource:
Soo Bahk Do® Institute Video Subscription For Your Target Rank

Cho Dan to E Dan | Promotion Requirements |

General Requirements
The following are minimum requirements to be eligible for promotion:
- Age requirements: No minimum age
- Proof of current federation membership (Federation ID Card)
- Membership time must equal or exceed required training time
- Must be of sound moral character

Expectations of Performance
Candidate should be able to demonstrate the following:
- Proper Moo Do Jaseh
- Connection of 8 Key Concepts
- Demonstrate Shim Gung, Neh Gung, and Weh Gung
- Demonstration of Shin Chook in movement

Culture, Terminology, and History
Candidate should be able to explain his or her understanding of the following:
- ***Written Essay Requirement # 1***
    - What does your Dan Bon mean to you and how does it relate to the Moo Duk Kwan and its discipline?
        - Minimum of 1000 words, typewritten and double spaced.
- ***Written Essay Requirement # 2***
    - Cite your personal Vision participation and Vision contributions that you have made during your training career and how they have helped achieve measurable success toward vision objectives.
        - 1 Page maximum typewritten document.
        - Effective 2019 WMDK has requested each Country to begin acquiring a signed "Consent To Publish" form from Dan essays authors. Those who grant permission may find their essay published on the web or elsewhere. (Examples) Your Dan Shim Sa application packet may be required to include a signed form denying or granting permission to publish your Dan Shim Sa Essays.

Cho Dan to E Dan | Demonstration of Ability |

HAND TECHNIQUES   SOO GI
Soo Bahk Do Gi Cho – Il Bon Techniques
Any lower rank material can be requested

FOOT TECHNIQUES   JOK GI
E Dan Ssang Bal Cha Gi
Any lower rank material can be requested

FORMS   HYUNG
Chil Sung Il Ro Hyung
Du Mun
Jin Do
Nai Han Ji E Dan

ONE / THREE STEP SPARRING   IL SOO SIK / SAM SOO SIK

Adults	Sam Soo Sik Classic *(demonstrate any 3)*
Children	Il Soo Sik: 1 – 17 *(odd numbers only)*

SELF-DEFENSE   HO SIN SUL

Adults	Lower Sleeve Grips Knife Defense (Dan Do)
Children	All Wrist Grips including Side and Back Knife Defense (Dan Do)

FREE SPARRING   JA YU DAE RYUN
Free Sparring

IN NEH   ENDURANCE
Ahp Bal Ahp Cha Nut Gi (lead/front leg) performed in Hu Gul Jaseh. Thirty (30) seconds on each side of continuous kicking with focus on power, speed and extension for maximum effectiveness of each kick. **Goal:** 40 kicks per leg.

BREAKING   KYOK PA
E Dan Ssang Bal Cha Gi (Double Jump Front Split Kick) or
Yeon Sok Kyok Pa with one Soo Gi and one Jok Gi technique performed simultaneously.
NOTE: *If the candidate cannot physically perform E Dan Ssang Bal Cha Gi, the Regional Examiner should be consulted prior to testing to define an acceptable break for completion of this requirement.*

Optional Study Resource:
Soo Bahk Do® Institute Video Subscription For Your Target Rank

E Dan to Sam Dan | Promotion Requirements |

General Requirements
The following are minimum requirements to be eligible for promotion:
- Age requirements: No minimum age
- Proof of current federation membership (Federation ID Card)
- Membership time must equal or exceed required training time
- Must be of sound moral character

Expectations of Performance
Candidate should be able to demonstrate the following:
- Proper Moo Do Jaseh
- Connection of 8 Key Concepts
- Demonstrate Shim Gung, Neh Gung, and Weh Gung
- Demonstration of proper line of technique combined with maximization of acceleration and speed

Culture, Terminology, and History
Candidate should be able to explain his or her understanding of the following:
- ***Written Essay Requirement # 1***
    - Describe the essential characteristics of Soo Bahk Do as taught in Moo Duk Kwan schools which make it unique and differentiate it from other styles. Candidate is requested to contemplate and expound upon the Moo Duk Kwan's uniqueness and accomplishments made from 1954 to 1961 in Korea. Vision Tour presentations have provided additional information about many of these events.
        - *Minimum of 1000 words, typewritten and double spaced.*
- ***Written Essay Requirement # 2***
    - Cite your personal Vision participation and Vision contributions that you have made during your training career and how they have helped achieve measurable success toward vision objectives.
        - *1 Page maximum typewritten document.*

        - *Effective 2019 WMDK has requested each Country to begin acquiring a signed "Consent To Publish" form from Dan essays authors. Those who grant permission may find their essay published on the web or elsewhere. (Examples) Your Dan Shim Sa application packet may be required to include a signed form denying or granting permission to publish your Dan Shim Sa Essays.*

E Dan to Sam Dan | Demonstration of Ability |

HAND TECHNIQUES / SOO GI
Soo Bahk Do Gi Cho – E Bon Techniques
Any lower rank material can be requested

FOOT TECHNIQUES / JOK GI
Low Front & Back Spinning Sweep – Ha Dan Ahp Hu Ri Gi / Ha Dan Dwi Hu Ri Gi
Any lower rank material can be requested

FORMS / HYUNG
Chil Sung Sam Ro Hyung
Joong Jul
Ro Hai
Nai Han Ji Sam Dan

ONE / THREE STEP SPARRING / IL SOO SIK / SAM SOO SIK
Jua Dae Ryun (Seated 1-Step Sparring)
Sam Soo Sik Yuk Ro *(demonstrate any 3 of the Yuk Ro inspired Sam Soo Sik)*
Note: Sam Soo Sik Classic to be instructed to Students who followed the Children's track up to this point (demonstrate any 3 of the Sam Soo Sik Classic).

SELF-DEFENSE / HO SIN SUL
Staff Defense (Jang Bong)
Mid-Sleeve Grips
Note: Lower Sleeve Grips to be instructed to Students who followed the Children's track up to this point.

FREE SPARRING / JA YU DAE RYUN
Double (2 on 1) Opponent Sparring | Da Soo In Dae Ryun

IN NEH / ENDURANCE
Ahp Cha Nut Gi (hopping), alternating each leg for thirty (30) seconds of continuous kicking. **Goal:** 50 kicks total with proper completion of each kick.

BREAKING / KYOK PA
Ro Hai Hyung with Break

Optional Study Resource:
Soo Bahk Do® Institute Video Subscription For Your Target Rank

Sam Dan to Sa Dan | Promotion Requirements |

General Requirements
The following are minimum requirements to be eligible for promotion:
- Minimum age requirements: 21 years old
- Proof of current federation membership (Federation ID Card)
- Membership time must equal or exceed required training time
- Must be of sound moral character

Expectations of Performance
Candidate should be able to demonstrate the following:
- Proper Moo Do Jaseh
- Connection of 8 Key Concepts
- Understanding and application in practice of Shim Gung, Neh Gung, and Weh Gung
- Demonstration of breath initiating Shin Chook connected with proper "chain of command"

Culture, Terminology, and History
Candidate should be able to explain his or her understanding of the following:
- ***Written Essay Requirement # 1***
    o Brief explanation of the Sip Sam Seh (including O-Heng and Pal Gwe) and what you have learned from it.
- ***Written Essay Requirement # 2***
    o History and meaning of required Hyung.

    o Effective 2019 WMDK has requested each Country to begin acquiring a signed "Consent To Publish" form from Dan essays authors. Those who grant permission may find their essay published on the web or elsewhere. (Examples) Your Dan Shim Sa application packet may be required to include a signed form denying or granting permission to publish your Dan Shim Sa Essays.

Sam Dan to Sa Dan | Demonstration of Ability |

HAND / FOOT TECHNIQUES — SOO GI / JOK GI
All Lower Belt Techniques and Requirements
Hand and Foot combinations using known techniques

FORMS — HYUNG
Chil Sung Sa Ro Hyung
Po Wol
Sip Soo
Kong Sang Koon

ONE / THREE STEP SPARRING — IL SOO SIK / SAM SOO SIK
All previous requirements to be demonstrated

SELF-DEFENSE — HO SIN SUL
All lower belt requirements

FREE SPARRING — JA YU DAE RYUN
All lower belt requirements
Jua Dae Ryun (Sparring in a Seated Position)
Wa Da Ryun (Sparring in a Lying Down Position)

BREAKING — KYOK PA
None

Optional Study Resource:
Soo Bahk Do® Institute Video Subscription For Your Target Rank

SA DAN TO O DAN | PROMOTION REQUIREMENTS |

General Requirements
The following are minimum requirements to be eligible for promotion:
- Minimum age requirements: 26 years old
- Proof of current federation membership (Federation ID Card)
- Membership time must equal or exceed required training time
- Must be of sound moral character

Expectations of Performance
Candidate should be able to demonstrate the following:
- Demonstrate proper connection of Shim Gung, Neh Gung and Weh Gung
- A personal and/or group demonstration of Moo Duk Kwan maturity and knowledge during the Ko Dan Ja Shim Sa

Culture, Terminology, and History
Candidate should be able to explain his or her understanding of the following:
- **Written Essay Requirement # 1**
    - Understanding of the Five Moo Do Values and their application in training.
- **Written Essay Requirement # 2**
    - History and meaning of required Hyung.

    - Effective 2019 WMDK has requested each Country to begin acquiring a signed "Consent To Publish" form from Dan essays authors. Those who grant permission may find their essay published on the web or elsewhere. (Examples) Your Dan Shim Sa application packet may be required to include a signed form denying or granting permission to publish your Dan Shim Sa Essays.

SA DAN TO O DAN | DEMONSTRATION OF ABILITY |

HAND / FOOT TECHNIQUES   SOO GI / JOK GI
All Lower Belt Techniques and Requirements
Hand and Foot combinations using known techniques

FORMS   HYUNG
Chil Sung O Ro Hyung
Yang Pyun
Sei Shan
Wang Shu

ONE / THREE STEP SPARRING   IL SOO SIK / SAM SOO SIK
All lower belt requirements

SELF-DEFENSE   HO SIN SUL
All lower belt requirements

FREE SPARRING   JA YU DAE RYUN
All lower belt requirements

BREAKING   KYOK PA
None

DEMONSTRATION
Candidate Group Demonstration of Moo Duk Kwan Maturity and Knowledge

Optional Study Resource:
Soo Bahk Do® Institute Video Subscription **For Your Target Rank**

O Dan to Yuk Dan | Promotion Requirements |

General Requirements
The following are minimum requirements to be eligible for promotion:
- Minimum age requirements: 32 years old
- Proof of current federation membership (Federation ID Card)
- Membership time must equal or exceed required training time
- Must be of sound moral character

Expectations of Performance
Candidate should be able to demonstrate the following:
- Visible leadership through Shim Gung, Neh Gung, and Weh Gung during the Ko Dan Ja Shim Sa
- Visible modeling and understanding of the Five Moo Do Values during the Ko Dan Ja Shim Sa
- A personal and/or group demonstration of Moo Duk Kwan maturity and knowledge during the Ko Dan Ja Shim Sa

Culture, Terminology, and History
Candidate should be able to explain his or her understanding of the following:
- ***Written Essay Requirement***
  - History and meaning of required Hyung.

  - *Effective 2019 WMDK has requested each Country to begin acquiring a signed "Consent To Publish" form from Dan essays authors. Those who grant permission may find their essay published on the web or elsewhere. (Examples) Your Dan Shim Sa application packet may be required to include a signed form denying or granting permission to publish your Dan Shim Sa Essays.*

O Dan to Yuk Dan | Demonstration of Ability |

HAND / FOOT TECHNIQUES   SOO GI / JOK GI
All Lower Belt Techniques and Requirements
Hand and Foot combinations using known techniques

FORMS   HYUNG
Chil Sung Yuk Ro Hyung
Sal Chu
Ji On
O Sip Sa Bo

ONE / THREE STEP SPARRING   IL SOO SIK / SAM SOO SIK
All lower belt requirements

SELF-DEFENSE   HO SIN SUL
All lower belt requirements

FREE SPARRING   JA YU DAE RYUN
All lower belt requirements

BREAKING   KYOK PA
None

DEMONSTRATION
Candidate Group Demonstration of Moo Duk Kwan Maturity and Knowledge

Optional Study Resource:
Soo Bahk Do® Institute Video Subscription **For Your Target Rank**

Yuk Dan to Chil Dan | Promotion Requirements |

General Requirements
The following are minimum requirements to be eligible for promotion:
- Minimum age requirements: 39 years old
- Proof of current federation membership (Federation ID Card)
- Membership time must equal or exceed required training time
- Must be of sound moral character

Pre-requisites for Participation:
- Seven (7) years active training since Yuk Dan promotion
- Participation in five (5) National Events (Moo Do Festival, etc.)
- Participation in one (1) International Event (KDJSS, Symposium, MDK Anniversary, etc.) held outside of your native country
- Member in good standing of and contribution to the World Moo Duk Kwan
- Sound moral character

Expectations of Performance
Candidate should be able to demonstrate the following:
- Demonstrate proper connection of Shim Gung, Neh Gung and Weh Gung
- Provide documented history of regional support on permanent member record and regional leadership activities

Culture, Terminology, and History
Candidate should be able to explain his or her understanding of the following:
- ***Written Essay Requirement***
    - History and meaning of required Hyung.

    - *Effective 2019 WMDK has requested each Country to begin acquiring a signed "Consent To Publish" form from Dan essays authors. Those who grant permission may find their essay published on the web or elsewhere. (Examples) Your Dan Shim Sa application packet may be required to include a signed form denying or granting permission to publish your Dan Shim Sa Essays.*

YUK DAN TO CHIL DAN | DEMONSTRATION OF ABILITY |

HAND / FOOT TECHNIQUES — SOO GI / JOK GI
All Lower Belt Techniques and Requirements
Hand and Foot combinations using known techniques

FORMS — HYUNG
Chil Sung Chil Ro Hyung
Choong Ro
Hwa Sun

ONE / THREE STEP SPARRING — IL SOO SIK / SAM SOO SIK
All lower belt requirements

SELF-DEFENSE — HO SIN SUL
All lower belt requirements

FREE SPARRING — JA YU DAE RYUN
All lower belt requirements

BREAKING — KYOK PA
None

DEMONSTRATION
Candidate Group Demonstration of Moo Duk Kwan Maturity and Knowledge

Optional Study Resource:
Soo Bahk Do® Institute Video Subscription **For Your Target Rank**

THE MOO DUK KWAN® DAN BON
By H.C. Hwang Kwan Jang Nim

"Dan Bon" simply means "Dan Number," however, that simple description does not reveal or convey the rich depth of tradition, history and meaning associated with the Moo Duk Kwan's Dan Bon system. The Moo Duk Kwan Dan Bon system is a very important and traditional part of the Moo Duk Kwan organization. It is a source of great personal pride for Soo Bahk Do practitioners embracing the Moo Duk Kwan and its philosophy. Today, I'd like to share a few of the very unique aspects of the Moo Duk Kwan Dan Bon system with you.

When the Founder, Hwang Kee founded the Moo Duk Kwan school in 1945, he began with just seven students. Only one student was successful at achieving the Cho Dan Rank after long, hard Moo Duk Kwan training. The late Master Un Chang Kim was about 30 years old when he earned Dan Bon #1 from The Founder, Hwang Kee in 1948. It was on that day the Moo Duk Kwan Dan Bon tradition was born. The last Dan Bon issued by Founder Hwang Kee in July of 2002 was 41208. As of 2019, over 50,000 Soo Bahk Do practitioners worldwide have earned their legitimate Moo Duk Kwan Dan Bon and their permanent place in its living history.

What makes the Moo Duk Kwan Dan Bon system so unique? It is the fact that the Dan Bon clearly defines each Dan holder's seniority and place within the Moo Duk Kwan rank system. The Dan Bon system was initiated and created based on a high value of loyalty, history, tradition, discipline, and philosophy. Once a Cho Dan receives their Dan Number, they keep it permanently. Their Dan Bon is not just an administration number. It signifies an important aspect of our Moo Do identity within the Moo Duk Kwan and designates our definite place in the Moo Duk Kwan rank system. At any National or International Moo Duk Kwan event, without discussion, without dispute or conflict, and without confusion, the Dan Bon system allows practitioners who may have never even met to harmoniously assume their rightful place in line among peers from around the world. Where else can you find this kind of Moo Do system like the Moo Duk Kwan has? Because Soo Bahk Do training is very disciplined, a strong meaning is attached to seniority and the Dan Bon reveals one's seniority within the Moo Duk Kwan, even among Dan practitioners you may never have met before. Many organizations may have member numbering systems for the purpose of administration; however, such numbers do not reflect a practitioner's Moo Do identity or represent the defining discipline of seniority.

Why is Dan Bon in our style treated so highly and respected as a symbol of seniority? There are several reasons:

- Hwang Kee, as the Founder of the system, initiated the Dan Bon system and was the only person who oversaw and authorized each Dan Bon based on the Moo Do seniority of each practitioner. He personally assigned Dan Bon numbers until his retirement. *(Editor's note: Founder Hwang Kee passed on the responsibility of protecting and preserving the integrity of the Moo Duk Kwan Dan Bon system to his designated successor, H. C. Hwang Kwan Jang Nim.)* To this day, the Moo Duk Kwan Dan Bon system remains continuous and unbroken since its inception.
- As a result of high level of discipline and training, the Grandmaster has taught the importance of seniority to all his students and the Grandmaster has linked their Moo Do seniority through the Dan Bon system.
- The Moo Duk Kwan was the most visible and well-known martial art in Korea until the early 1960s. The Founder's teachings and his student's demonstrations of respect for the Dan Bon system made profound impacts on the martial arts society during that period of time.

The following are a few incidents that exemplify the importance of Dan Bon within our system and outside our system and will provide you with a deeper understanding of the Moo Duk Kwan Dan Bon seniority system.

1. In the early 1960's after the military coup (birth of Tae Kwon Do in Korea), the Moo Duk Kwan was divided. Many Moo Duk Kwan practitioners joined the Tae Kwon Do Association for political reasons. At that time, even though they were outside of Soo Bahk Do Moo Duk Kwan, some practitioners tried to steal and destroy the Kwan Jok Bu (the book of the list of Dan Bon) in order to erase the record of seniority from the Moo Duk Kwan. In this way, they believed that they could pass off as senior members with political influence. This attempt failed.

2. In United States history, when senior instructors of Tang Soo Do / Soo Bahk Do Moo Duk Kwan broke away to form their own organization, some attempted to copy the Dan Bon system by issuing numbers to students that continued from the last Dan Bon that had been issued by

Founder Hwang Kee rather than starting from #1 for their own organization's practitioners.

3. Among many Moo Duk Kwan alumni throughout the world, regardless of their present affiliation, they still publicize their Moo Duk Kwan Dan Bon received from the Founder Hwang Kee as they attempt to enhance their credibility and establish the origin of their Moo Do identity. These realities are examples of the profound impact that the Moo Duk Kwan Dan Bon has had on the martial arts community worldwide.

We have the opportunity to protect and preserve this unique and proud tradition by continuing to practice the same values that originated the Dan Bon system. Our tradition has not been lost. All Dan Bon holders stem from the same roots. We can each trace our origin as Dan members directly back to Founder Hwang Kee and our Dan Bon confirms that fact.

To be loyal, to maintain one's connection to the source of one's Moo Do identity, that is the essence of the Moo Duk Kwan. Those who forfeit their connection lose the compass of their martial art journey and their Shim Gung is lost.

THE MOO DUK KWAN® KO DAN JA SHIM SA FOR SOO BAHK DO®

The Moo Duk Kwan® Ko Dan Ja Shim Sa is unique in the martial arts world and provides a premiere training and learning experience for all participants. Only members in good standing who are classing eligible and/or time eligible shall be considered for eligibility to test for Moo Duk Kwan® Ko Dan Ja rank certification (4th Dan and up) and/or Kyo Bom / Sa Bom Certification in the U.S.

United States Soo Bahk Do Moo Duk Kwan Federation® members who respond to an initial eligibility questionnaire and who are subsequently recommended and invited to an annual U.S. Ko Dan Ja Shim Sa are joined at the event by other qualified applicants, guests and Alumni as may be invited.

Pursuant to the Technical Advisory Committee's directives & Federation policies:
- Members planning to apply for Kyo Bom or Sa Bom Certification when testing for Ko Dan Ja Rank must acquire and possess a Certification Study Kit prior to their Ko Dan Ja Shim Sa and Kyo Bom or Sa Bom Certification Exam date.
- Applicants for instructor certification over age 18 must have an active Background Check & Continuing Education subscription on the Soo Bahk Do Institute
    - Successfully completed a Background Check
    - Completed Safety training
- Applicants for Kyo Bom or Sa Bom Certification must have been previously certified as a Kyo Sa.
- Applicants for Associate Kyo Bom do not need to have been previously certified as a Kyo Sa.
- The TAC requires that all Sa Bom Certification applicants who participate in a Sa Bom Certification exam at a Ko Dan Ja Shim Sa shall also be required to undergo an extended self-evaluation period after the Ko Dan Ja Shim Sa experience in order to complete their Sa Bom Certification.
- Members planning to apply for Sa Bom Certification in their future should pro-actively plan ahead and complete the pre-requisite requirements for Sa Bom Certification eligibility well before being eligible or invited to test for Ko Dan Ja rank.
- Members eligible for Ko Dan Ja rank who have not previously completed the required years of Jo Kyo and Kyo Sa certification may be ineligible to apply for Sa Bom; however, members with comparable life experience may be allowed to request TAC consideration and such requests will be reviewed by the TAC on a case by case basis.

OVERVIEW OF THE KO DAN JA SHIM SA PROCESS

Once per year, all classing eligible and time eligible current U.S. Federation members are identified.

A letter of notification of their eligibility and a questionnaire are sent to all eligible U.S. Federation members.

Questionnaire Recipients are extended an opportunity to indicate their preference for testing location, and some may elect to test at an international Ko Dan Ja Shim Sa.

Questionnaire Recipients who return their completed questionnaire by the deadline are then submitted to various Federation Officials for recommendations.

Questionnaire Respondents who receive a majority of positive recommendations from Federation Officials are then sent a formal invitation to test for Ko Dan Ja Rank along with paperwork requirements and event registration materials that must be submitted by the deadline.

Invited Candidates who fulfill the paperwork and registration requirements are then scheduled to attend and participate in the week long, once per year Ko Dan Ja Shim Sa where they complete their Ko Dan Ja Rank testing requirements.

In the U.S., the TAC Chair also extends a standing invitation to all Ko Dan Ja Alumni to participate in the week-long training and Ko Dan Ja Shim Sa experience as visitors.

The history of the U.S. Ko Dan Ja Shim Sa is a long and proud one and since 2000 the Federation has also hosted **A Moment With The Masters** in conjunction with the 1st weekend of the Ko Dan Ja Shim Sa.

During the Moment With The Masters, fellow members have an opportunity to share a few moments with the wave of new KDJ hopefuls and current KDJ leaders participating in the week-long Ko Dan Ja Shim Sa experience.

Additional Ko Dan Ja Shim Sa & Moment With The Masters Info:
https://kdjss.soobahkdo.org/

INSTRUCTOR CERTIFICATION OVERVIEW

Motivated members who would like to take their passion for Soo Bahk Do® to the next level and help change people's lives in a positive way are invited to explore the rewards and opportunities of instructor certification.

Only a very few high achieving members successfully attain Jo Ko, Kyo Sa, Kyo Bom or Sa Bom Certification and if you are inspired to pursue any of those personal goals, your personal instructor and your Federation are here to support your success. Speak to your personal instructor about your goals regarding Instructor Certification to review your readiness, rewards and opportunities.

When you are certified as a Jo Kyo, Kyo Sa, Kyo Bom or Sa Bom, you assume the exciting and rewarding role of passing our art on from instructor to student and in doing so you positively change students' lives and you assure our art's preservation for future generations.

As a Moo Duk Kwan® certified Instructor you will be authorized to represent the Founder Hwang Kee's Soo Bahk Do® martial art system, providing your membership is kept current, your certification is kept current, you maintain an active Background Check and Continuing Education subscription on the Soo Bahk Do Institute and you fulfill all administrative responsibilities and maintain and upgrade your technical and instructional skills in accordance with the Federation's published expectations.

Certified Instructors are granted a limited license for non-commercial use of the Soo Bahk Do® service marks and Moo Duk Kwan® trademarks, and associated copyrighted materials and permission to teach all the intellectual property comprising the Soo Bahk Do® martial art system in accordance with Moo Duk Kwan® standards.

As a certified instructor, you assume a very important Technical Responsibility to represent Soo Bahk Do® techniques and the Moo Duk Kwan® philosophy of the Kwan Jang Nim's martial art system in an exemplary manner that will preserve the purity of the art.

Certified instructors are expected to follow the guidance of the Technical Advisory Committee with respect to all technical, historical and philosophical material and to participate in at least two (2) Regional and/or National Federation events each year and to maintain an active Background Check and Continuing Education subscription on the Soo Bahk Do® Institute as two requirements for maintaining your certification in good standing.

Certified Instructors are expected to demonstrate the highest level of Administrative Responsibility by becoming familiar with the Charter and By-laws of the United States Soo Bahk Do Moo Duk Kwan Federation® and following the administrative guidelines of the Board of Directors, including, but not limited to, encouraging and assuring all your students become Federation members prior to testing them.

Certified Instructors sign an oath to test only students with current Federation membership for rank promotion.

It is each certified instructor's responsibility to request and confirm current membership status before testing a student for rank promotion.

It is each student's responsibility to provide proof of membership to their instructor before a rank test.

Certification Maintenance

Certification is a credential granted by an external organization or company confirming that an individual has specific skills in a certain area.

Certifications are typically time limited and expire due to the constantly evolving nature of skills required in today's world. Certifications, driver's licenses, etc. can be extended, renewed and maintained in good standing when the holder completes the maintenance or renewal requirements as specified by the certifying organization.

The Moo Duk Kwan® philosophy of continual growth, development, and improvement is clearly evident in the Moo Duk Kwan rank system and in keeping with that philosophy and the dynamic and evolving nature of our living art and modern society, Certified Instructors and Certified Do Jang Owners can best lead the way for the long term preservation of Soo Bahk Do Moo Duk Kwan by continually refining and updating instructor skills and entrepreneurial acumen to be as effective as possible in our fast paced and constantly changing society.

The United States Soo Bahk Do Moo Duk Kwan Federation® supports continuing education and advancement for all members wanting to pursue Instructor Certification and Do Jang ownership because of their crucial role in the preservation of our living art.

Effective 01/01/2019 Certified Instructors are required to maintain an active subscription to the Background Check and Continuing Education subscription on the Soo Bahk Do Institute in order to maintain the privileges associated with, and available to, certified Instructors.

Instructor Certification Timelines

Instructor Certification	* Minimum * Study Kit Possession & Apprenticeship Time	Certification Requirements
Jo Kyo	90 days	Minimum Age: 10 years old Minimum Rank: 3rd Gup (Red Belt)
Kyo Sa	1 year	Proof of previous Jo Kyo Certification Minimum Age: 18 years old Minimum Rank: Cho Dan (1st Dan)
Kyo Bom	1 year	Minimum Age: 21 years old Minimum Rank: Sa Dan (4th Dan)
Sa Bom	2 years	Proof of Jo Kyo and Kyo Sa Certification Minimum Age: 25 years old Minimum Rank: Sa Dan (4th Dan)

Instructor Certification Overview

Instructor Certification	JO KYO	KYO SA	KYO BOM	KYO BOM	SA BOM
Salutation	Jo Kyo Nim	Kyo Sa Nim	Kyo Bom Nim	Kyo Bom Nim	Sa Bom Nim
Rank Eligibility	3rd Gup	Cho Dan	Sa Dan	Sa Dan	Sa Dan
Minimum Age	10	18	21	21	25
Minimum Duration to Maintain Study Kit	90 Days	1 year	1 year	1 year	2 years
Prerequisites	None	Jo Kyo Certified	None	Kyo Sa Certified or Apprentice for Kyo Sa	Kyo Sa Certified or Kyo Bom Certified (Optional)
Rank Recommendation Authority	None	Gup & Dan	None	Gup & Dan	Gup / Dan / Ko Dan Ja
Testing Board Presence	May sit for Gup Tests, but may not conduct Examination nor submit rank recommendation.	May conduct & sit on Gup Exam Boards. May recommend students for Dan, but may not sit on Dan Exam Boards.	May sit on Gup Exam Boards, but may not conduct Examination nor submit rank recommendation. NOTE: Supervising Sa Bom may support rank recommendations.	May sit on Gup & Dan Exam boards and submit Gup & Dan rank recommendations.	May conduct and sit on Gup/Dan/KDJ Exam Boards and submit Gup/Dan/Ko Dan Ja rank recommendations.

Additional Instructor Certification Info:
https://soobahkdo.biz/how-do-i-become-a-moo-duk-kwan-certified-instructor/

Introduction to Kyo Bom

Kyo Bom is a term that has its composition familiar to the membership. "Kyo" is translated as "Teach", and "Bom" is translated as "Law or Pattern." In Korea during the 1940s, when there were a smaller number of Dan members, the term Kyo Bom was used to refer to senior members with teaching responsibilities. As the art expanded globally and the number of Dan and Ko Dan Ja members increased, the use of Kyo Bom fell out of common practice.

The intent of this program is to connect with our History and reintroduce the term Kyo Bom to support the growth and development of Sa Dan candidates, who while not pursuing Sa Bom certification in some cases, still carry the responsibility to effectively communicate the teachings of Soo Bahk Do as direct representatives of the Founder and Kwan Jang Nim. This is particularly the case as an increasing number of Youth Leaders are reaching Sa Dan eligibility before the current age requirement of 25 years old for Sa Bom certification.

The foundation for Kyo Bom certification currently exists within the specialized training that all Sa Dan candidates currently participate in today by producing teaching videos, instruction from TAC and Senior Leaders on principles of advanced teaching, reviewing specialized teaching content in the Ko Dan Ja Shim Sa Workbooks and by actual instruction during the Ko Dan Ja testing week.

Kyo Bom includes the following two certification levels:

- Associate Kyo Bom - Kyo Bom who have not previously achieved Jo Kyo and Kyo Sa certification. These members are high-level practitioners who represent the art of Soo Bahk Do® in accordance with Moo Duk Kwan® standards and expectations of an individual practitioner and who can successfully teach and convey the art to students in individual classes. They may sit on Gup Testing boards and can administer promotions at the Yu Gup Ja level under the supervised direction of a Sa Bom.

- Kyo Bom - Kyo Bom who have achieved Jo Kyo and Kyo Sa certification. They have all of the qualities of both Jo Kyo and Kyo Sa, but have also proven to be a high level practitioner (Ko Dan Ja). With a higher level of personal understanding and ability to perform, these members can successfully mentor both Yu Gup Ja and Yu Dan Ja members. Additionally, they can independently administer promotions at the Gup and Dan levels.

    - ***NOTE:*** Sa Bom certification is still an option for Sa Dan candidates that meet the minimum age requirement (25 years) and other prerequisites. Members that wish to receive Sa Bom certification along with their Sa Dan examination will still be required to complete the Jo Kyo and Kyo Sa certification process.

Additional Kyo Bom Certification Info:
https://soobahkdo.biz/kyo-bom-certification/

Jo Kyo Certification

Certification Requirements
The following are minimum requirements to be eligible for Jo Kyo Certification:
- Minimum Age:
    - 10 years old
- Minimum Rank:
    - 3rd Gup (Red Belt)
- Minimum Training Time:
    - 90 days following acquisition of Jo Kyo Study Kit
    - **NOTE:** Jo Kyo Study Kit may be ordered at any rank

Eligibility
- Instructor's recommendation required to test
- Consult Do Jang Owner
- Age 18 and above, active **Background Check & Continuing Education Subscription** on the Soo Bahk Do® Institute
    - Successful Background Check
    - Completed Safety Training Course
- Completed Jo Kyo Study Kit
- Completed Apprenticeship Log
- Completed Application Form
- Proof of Current Federation Membership (Federation ID Card)

Examination Process
- Jo Kyo Certification Exams are typically conducted in a Certified Do Jang by your personal instructor.

Order Study Kit & More Info:
https://soobahkdo.biz/how-do-i-become-a-moo-duk-kwan-certified-instructor/

Kyo Sa Certification

Certification Requirements
The following are minimum requirements to be eligible for Kyo Sa Certification:
- Proof of previous Jo Kyo Certification
- Minimum Age:
    - 18 years old
- Minimum Rank:
    - 1st Dan (Cho Dan)
- Minimum Training Time:
    - 1 year following acquisition of Kyo Sa Study Kit
    - *NOTE:* Kyo Sa Study Kit may be ordered at any rank

Eligibility
- Instructor's recommendation required to test
- Consult Do Jang Owner
- Consult Regional Examiners
- Active **Background Check & Continuing Education Subscription** on the Soo Bahk Do® Institute
    - Successful Background Check
    - Completed Safety Training Course
- Completed Kyo Sa Study Kit
- Completed Apprenticeship Log
- Completed Application Form
- Proof of Current Federation Membership (Federation ID Card)

Examination Process
- Kyo Sa Certification Exams may be conducted at the Certified Do Jang Level, Regionally or Nationally pursuant to TAC instructions.

Order Study Kit & More Info:
https://soobahkdo.biz/how-do-i-become-a-moo-duk-kwan-certified-instructor/

Kyo Bom Certification

Certification Requirements
The following are minimum requirements to be eligible for Kyo Bom Certification:
- **Associate Kyo Bom:**
    - No previous instructor certifications required
- **Kyo Bom:**
    - Proof of previous Kyo Sa Certification
- Minimum Age:
    - 21 years old
- Minimum Rank:
    - 4th Dan (Sa Dan)
- Minimum Training Time:
    - 1 Year following acquisition of Kyo Bom Study Kit
    - **NOTE:** Kyo Bom Study Kit may be ordered at any rank

Eligibility
- Instructor's recommendation required to test
- Consult Do Jang Owner
- Active **Background Check & Continuing Education Subscription** on the Soo Bahk Do® Institute
    - Successful Background Check
    - Completed Safety Training Course
- Completed Kyo Bom Study Kit
- Completed Apprenticeship Log
- Completed Application Form
- Proof of Current Federation Membership (Federation ID Card)

Examination Process
- Eligible members may apply to test for Kyo Bom Certification when invited to test for Sa Dan rank at the Ko Dan Ja Shim Sa

Order Study Kit & More Info:
https://soobahkdo.biz/how-do-i-become-a-moo-duk-kwan-certified-instructor/

Sa Bom Certification

Certification Requirements
The following are minimum requirements to be eligible for Sa Bom Certification:
- Proof of previous Kyo Sa and/or **Kyo Bom** Certification
    - Minimum Age: 25 years old
    - Minimum Rank: 4th Dan (Sa Dan)
- Minimum Training Time:
    - 2 Years following acquisition of Sa Bom Study Kit
    - *NOTE:* Sa Bom Study Kit may be acquired at any rank

Eligibility
- Instructor's recommendation required to test
- Consult Do Jang Owner
- Active **Background Check & Continuing Education Subscription** on the Soo Bahk Do® Institute
    - Successful Background Check
    - Completed Safety Training Course
- Completed Sa Bom Study Kit
- Completed Apprenticeship Log
- Completed Application Form
- Proof of Current Federation Membership (Federation ID Card)

Examination Process
- Eligible members may apply to test for Sa Bom Certification when invited to test for Sa Dan rank at the Ko Dan Ja Shim Sa
    - *NOTE:* Members eligible for Ko Dan Ja rank who have not previously completed the required years of Jo Kyo and Kyo Sa certification may be ineligible to apply for Sa Bom; however, members with comparable life experience may be allowed to request TAC consideration and such requests will be reviewed by the TAC on a case by case basis.
- Eligible members may also apply to test for Sa Bom Certification in any subsequent year between Ko Dan Ja rank promotions
- Potential Sa Bom Certification Applicants (Sa Bom Study Kit Holders) are notified by TAC each year of Sa Bom Certification Examination opportunities and receive paperwork submission instructions / registration information from TAC
- Sa Bom Certification Exams are conducted nationally at the annual Ko Dan Ja Shim Sa pursuant to TAC instructions

Order Study Kit & More Info:
https://soobahkdo.biz/how-do-i-become-a-moo-duk-kwan-certified-instructor/

Rank Promotion Process

Gup Promotion Procedures

In the U.S. Federation a Certified Instructor operating a Certified School assumes responsibility for teaching the art of Soo Bahk Do® in accordance with Moo Duk Kwan® standards and to periodically test their student members for rank promotion. Successful test recommendations acknowledging a student's progress are to be submitted to National Member Headquarters within 10 days of an exam so they can be forwarded to the TAC and then the Kwan Jang Nim.

When an instructor submits a Gup rank certification recommendation for a student through the TAC to the Kwan Jang Nim and it is approved, then the Kwan Jang Nim authorizes Gup rank certification be issued to the student member. A Gup rank certificate will be produced and delivered from Headquarters to the student's instructor for ceremonial award to the student in front of their peers as specified by the TAC.

The credibility and integrity of the Moo Duk Kwan® ranking system is preserved by Certified Instructors who proudly demonstrate the discipline and respect for the rank certification process as established by the Kwan Jang Nim and preserved by the TAC and the U.S. Federation.

1. Only a Kyo Sa, Kyo Bom or Sa Bom Certified Instructor operating a certified school can test students and forward a rank recommendation to the Chairman of the T.A.C. for students.
2. Prior to a Gup Test, students are to furnish proof of Federation membership to their instructor and complete an *"Application for Gup Promotion."* It is the responsibility of the student to possess a Federation ID card and to complete the testing form.
3. It is the responsibility of the Instructor to confirm current membership status of all applicants BEFORE testing them.
4. It is not necessary to notify the Federation of a Gup testing in advance, but Instructors are required to submit all testing results and recommendations for students to Headquarters within ten (10) days of the test date. You must conduct your tests according to the standards of the T.A.C. of the United States Soo Bahk Do Moo Duk Kwan Federation
5. Following a testing, you are to retain on file the completed copies of all "Applications for Gup Promotion" for each student. Each student's forms are to be available at the location where the student trains for a period of four years or until Dan rank is achieved.
6. Following each testing, you are to compile and send to Headquarters a listing of all Gup rank promotion recommendations for your students

from the completed *"Applications for Gup Promotion."* Use the *"Group Test Form"* provided by Headquarters for this purpose.
7. It is important that these forms be used and instructions be followed carefully to ensure prompt processing of your student's Gup rank promotions.
8. Be certain that you include your school certification number as well as the Gup identification number for each student on the "Group Test Form."
9. Send the completed *"Group Test Form"* to Headquarters using one of the following methods:
    a. **Via U.S. Mail:** PROMOTION, U.S. Soo Bahk Do Moo Duk Kwan Federation, 20 Millburn Ave, Floor 2, Springfield, NJ 07081
    b. **Via FAX:** (973) 467-5716
    c. **Via Email:** GupTests@soobahkdo.com
10. Upon receipt of your completed "Group Test Form" at Headquarters, the membership status will be confirmed for all students you have recommended for Gup rank promotion. Non-members and non-current members will not be processed. You and the student will be notified.
11. All students with current membership status will be forwarded to the T.A.C. for approval of your Gup rank promotion recommendations. After T.A.C. approval, the Membership Committee will then process the student's rank certificates and forward them to you for prompt distribution to the students.

Dan Promotion Procedures

Kyo Sa, Kyo Bom or Sa Bom Certified Instructors operating certified schools may recommend applicants for Dan rank to Appointed Regional Testing Boards for Dan Rank Promotion. Regional Testing Boards are available to Federation Members twice a year and, following the candidate's demonstration before the testing board, a rank promotion recommendation by the Testing Board is forwarded to the T.A.C. Chairman for final approval by the Kwan Jang Nim. Once approved, a legitimate Moo Duk Kwan® rank certificate is forwarded to the member's instructor for ceremonial presentation.
Regional Testing Boards shall be appointed by the Chairman of the T.A.C.
1. Only T.A.C. appointed Regional Testing Boards can administer a Dan rank test for students. Traditionally, there are two (2) official Dan Shim Sa events each year, one cycle in the spring and the other in the fall.
2. Prior to a Dan Test, students shall complete a *"WMDK Application For Dan Rank Promotion Form,"* and other written requirements as specified by the T.A.C. in this manual and the official announcement package. Each applicant, who has been recommended by his/her instructor, will submit the following items to his/her instructor before the specified deadline:

a. Dan test application form (typewritten)
   b. Required essay
   c. Photocopy of current Federation membership card
   d. Photocopy of current rank certificate
   e. Dan Shim Sa fee
3. It is the Instructor's and School Owner's responsibility to confirm and certify that all applicants they recommend meet all the minimum TAC requirements PRIOR TO recommending any applicants for the requested rank and PRIOR TO submission of applicant packages.
4. It is the responsibility of the designated Regional Examiner to review and confirm that applicants meet all the minimum TAC requirements for the requested rank PRIOR TO rank testing and PRIOR TO applicant's participation in a Dan Shim Sa.
5. Any applicant that does not meet the minimum TAC requirements for the requested Dan rank must have prior written authorization from the TAC Chair, and a copy of such written authorization must be obtained and attached by the applicant's instructor to the applicant's Application for Dan Rank Promotion Form.
6. Instructors are to submit the applicant's packet and appropriate fees to the Regional Administrator by their Region's specified deadline.
7. The Regional Testing Board will confirm the current membership status of all applicants, that they meet all the TAC minimum requirements and that any required TAC Chair authorization letters are obtained BEFORE testing them.
8. After completion of Dan Testing, there will be a meeting of the Regional Testing Board to evaluate the recommendations for each candidate before submission to the Chairman of T.A.C.
9. Recommendation of the Regional Testing Board will be sent to the Chairman of T.A.C., along with appropriate fees from the Regional Administrator to Federation Headquarters.
10. Upon approval by the Chairman of T.A.C., recommendations for promotion and certification fees will be forwarded to the Kwan Jang Nim. Dan rank certificates approved by the Kwan Jang Nim will be sent from Federation Headquarters to the candidate's instructor. If the T.A.C. or Kwan Jang Nim do not approve the test recommendations, the Regional Examining Board, the recommending instructor and the candidate will be notified with reasons for rejection no later than one month after the testing date.

Obtaining School Certification

1. You must be a Certified Instructor or must plan to operate under the direct guidance of a Certified Instructor who will commit to supervising your activity at the location where you intend to offer instruction.

2. Every Certified School (Do Jang) must have at least one Kyo Sa, Kyo Bom or Sa Bom Certified Instructor teaching a majority of the classes at the location because they are the only ones authorized to instruct Soo Bahk Do®. In special cases, the T.A.C. may approve uncertified assistants or uncertified transfer Instructors to serve in this capacity if they are involved in an ongoing Instructor training program under the supervision of a Certified Instructor.

3. Each physical location where students receive instruction must be certified even when the supervising Certified Instructor already has other certified locations. Each location where Soo Bahk Do® instruction is taking place must be on record with the Federation for proper distribution of member information.

4. You begin by obtaining / downloading a School Certification Kit from the website which contains specific forms and information about operating a Certified School and the requirements associated with certification. It also outlines some ways the Federation may be able to assist you in establishing your new school so that you can enjoy the most rewarding instructional experience possible while your students enjoy the highest quality training environment available.

5. The School Certification Kit includes an *"Announcement of Intent"* form and *"Letters of Notification,"* which help inform Headquarters and the two closest Certified Federation Schools of your intentions to open a school. These forms should be completed and submitted to Headquarters with the associated application fee while adhering to the proper guidelines explained in your kit BEFORE any instruction is performed at the proposed location.

6. Upon receipt of these forms and pursuant to School Certification guidelines, the T.A.C. will issue a "Pending Certification Status" for your proposed location.

7. In the case of transfer schools, the School Certification process is the same as specified in the School Certification Kit.

8. Once the specific location has been established and the school owner's and head instructor's relationships with the students at the location have been defined, then a formal *"Application for School Certification"* (included in School Certification Kit) must be completed and returned to Headquarters. Read it carefully, as obtaining School Certification entails accepting serious responsibilities to the member students you instruct as well as to the Kwan Jang Nim, the art and your Federation.

9. You will be required to have certain items displayed and available at your Do Jang as well as to demonstrate satisfactory understanding and etiquette to the Regional Examiner who performs a visitation before certification is issued. These specific requirements related to completing the School Certification process will be furnished to you with your School Certification Kit.

10. You may be required to address certain deficient areas before a specified deadline and certification will be held until the requirements are satisfied. During the time your certification is pending, you will be instructed to remit certification fees and other paperwork as required. Once full certification is issued, Gup fees no longer have to be remitted with rank promotion recommendations.

Download School Certification Applications & More Info:
https://soobahkdo.biz/how-do-i-become-a-moo-duk-kwan-school-owner/

Transfers from Outside the Federation

The United States Soo Bahk Do Moo Duk Kwan Federation® welcomes any students training in other martial art styles and organizations to join the Moo Duk Kwan family. Decisions regarding transfers reside with the instructor's judgment and experience based on the Moo Duk Kwan® standards.

In order to be transferred from a different style to a specific rank, the transfer student should be able to demonstrate all previous and current requirements for that level. All applications and physical examinations will be evaluated according to the highest level of Moo Duk Kwan® standards for Soo Bahk Do® at a recognized Certified Do Jang and/or a Federation Regional Dan Shim Sa event and ultimately approved by the Chairman of T.A.C.

Procedures for Gup members transferring from other styles or from an unaffiliated school:

Individuals of Gup rank coming from other styles should join the Federation immediately (transfer students do not need to identify a specific rank to become a member of the Federation). The transfer student should be encouraged to join the Soo Bahk Do® Institute to support the transition and learning process.

When the individual is ready to test, you (as determined by the certified instructor at a certified Do Jang) then the student may be recommended for promotion to the level you feel they are capable. However, if you are recommending a Gup rank promotion higher than 7th Gup, you must submit (via e-mail) a letter of recommendation explaining his/her qualifications along with a summary of their previous rank certifications (including scanned copies/pictures of rank certificates) to the Chairman of T.A.C. (tacchair@soobahkdo.com) for review and approval.

Procedures for Dan members transferring from other styles or from an unaffiliated school:

Individuals of Dan rank from other styles of martial arts who seek to transfer in as a Dan Member in to the Federation and the World Moo Duk Kwan must first apply for Federation membership (a specific rank is not required to initially become a member of the Federation). Joining the Soo Bahk Do® Institute will support the transition process as well.

At the Dan Level, in most cases, a transfer student would need to test for Cho Dan at a sanctioned Regional Dan Shim Sa in order to receive Dan certification regardless of their Dan rank from their previous style. However, there may be special circumstances that necessitate an alternate approach. As a result, the transfer student's personal instructor needs to consult with their Regional Examiner to define a plan for the transfer student's certification. The Regional Examiner will then need to submit (via e-mail) the suggested certification plan, a letter of recommendation explaining the transfer student's qualifications along with a summary of their previous rank certifications (including scanned copies/pictures of rank certificates) to the Chairman of T.A.C. (tacchair@soobahkdo.com) for review and approval of the plan.

Competition Overview & Tournament Rules

General Requirements
1. All contestants must be members in good standing of the United States Soo Bahk Do Moo Duk Kwan Federation®
2. All contestants must be dressed in traditional Moo Duk Kwan® manner. All uniforms must be cleaned, pressed and in good condition. The appropriate color trim must be worn according to each contestant's Gup or Dan rank in Soo Bahk Do®.
3. All members of the U.S. Federation must be wearing the approved Federation uniform patch. The patch must be worn on the left side of the uniform near the heart.

Official Opening and Closing Ceremony
1. The head referee and four corner judges should line up in a "seating seniority" format (alternating from most senior) rather than the standard seniority line like the contestants will be lined up in. The order is as follows - 2nd senior on the head referee's left, 3rd senior on head referee's right and so on (facing contestants).
2. The head referee, judges and contestants will then face (standing) the head table.
3. The head referee will call everyone to attention and bow in to the senior members at the head table.
4. The judges will then turn and face the contestants. The most senior contestant will call to attention and bow in to the judges.
5. The head referee will then call the contestants and judges to be seated for the start of the competition.
6. The Closing Ceremony follows the same format as above once the competition has been completed.

Hyung Competition
- Competitors will demonstrate one Hyung that meets their rank division requirements.
- There will be five judges for each form contest. Each judge will issue scores according to the following system:
    - Average Scores for each Rank
        - Gup Members: 7.7
        - Dan Members: 8.5
        - Ko Dan Ja Members: 9.3
- Scores from each of the five judges are recorded. The high and low score are removed from the average to calculate the final score for each competitor.

- During Hyung Competition, if a competitor makes a mistake during his/her performance (regardless of rank), the head referee should:
    - Give the competitor one more chance to perform the Hyung.
    - Deduct ½ point from the overall score.
    - For children, it is up to the judges' discretion to allow the competitor to start over from the beginning of the Hyung or to allow the child to start from the point of the mistake.
    - In the event that the competitor makes another mistake in the Hyung performance, disqualify the competitor from Hyung Competition.
- During Hyung Competition, if there is a tie score between competitors, the judges should:
    - Add back in the high and low scores that were omitted and compare the final score average.
    - If there still remains a tie between competitors, the judges should have the competitors demonstrate a second Hyung (should be different from the first Hyung that they performed).
        - If the competitor is not prepared to demonstrate another Hyung, he/she automatically drops to the next place.
        - *NOTE:* Each competitor should be prepared to demonstrate two different Hyung (regardless of age or rank).
    - The judges will score the Hyung performance by the standard points system, omitting the high and low scores to the overall score.
    - If there still remains a tie between the competitors, the judges should add back in the high and low scores that were omitted and compare the new final score average.
    - If there still remains a tie between the competitors, the judges should have the competitors demonstrate either one of the previous Hyung performed. It is the competitor's choice of which Hyung he/she will demonstrate.
        - The judges will then choose a winner by a show of hands.
- **Performance Criteria for Judging Hyung**
    - Proper Soo Bahk Do Hyung Sequence
    - Power Control
    - Tension and Relaxation
    - Speed and Rhythm Control
    - Direction of Movement
    - Spirit or Attitude
    - Proper Power of Techniques
    - Understanding Hyung Technique
    - Distinctive Features of Hyung
    - Perfect Finish
    - Precision of Movements / Chain of Command
    - Intentness
    - Proper Breathing Control
    - Ring Protocol Set by the Federation

- **Contestant's Etiquette for Hyung Competition Procedures**
    - When a contestant's name is called, they should stand up and walk to the edge of the ring.
    - The first person called should stand to the judges left, the 2nd person called should stand to the judges right.
    - Without further command, both contestants should bow simultaneously in to the judges / ring to show respect for the contest.
    - The contestants will then walk in to the Hyung starting position in the ring and bow to the judges (without commands).
    - The contestant on the left will then state only his/her name and the name of the Hyung while standing in Jhoon Bee position, the contestant on the right will follow.
    - After identifying themselves and their Hyung, and upon receiving the center judge's starting signal, the contestants will start performing their Hyung.
    - Upon completion of the Hyung, each contestant will return to Ba Ro (on their own, without commands) and await their scores.
    - After receiving their scores, the contestants will bow towards the judging panel.
    - The contestants will then step backwards (without turning their back to the judges) until reaching the edge of the ring and then will bow out to the judges followed by "Soo Bahk!"
    - Both contestants will turn towards each other, bow and shake hands as a sign of respect and good sportsmanship.

Traditional Point Sparring Competition

Point Sparring competition is a non-contact event. However, to ensure the safety of each competitor, all sparring participants must wear the following: headgear, mouthpiece, groin cup (men) & hand pads (covering knuckles only – must be white cloth). Full hand, foot and body protective gear is prohibited (shin pads are acceptable – white cloth only, but pads cannot be covering the feet). Fingernails and toenails should be cut to assure no cutting or scratching will occur due to jagged or long nails. No jewelry can be worn during free sparring.
- The match is officiated by one referee and four corner judges.
- Red and White Flags are used to signify each contestant in the ring.
- Each match is two minutes.
- Target Areas: Front portion of the body (above the belt and the face, from the top of the forehead down and from the ears forward (back of the head and top of the head are illegal target areas). Scoring on the line of any boundary area is considered a fair score.
- *Scoring a Point*
    - All basic hand and foot techniques to the allowable target areas are 1 point.
    - Any spinning or jumping kick (trailing leg above opponent's knee) is worth 2 points.

- - o A sidestep or a defensive Kyo Cha Rip Jaseh (cross-legged stance) with a counter attack is 2 points.
  - o A jump spinning technique with the base leg above the opponent's belt is 3 points.
- When the center referee stops the match once a call is communicated, each judge casts a vote.
- There must be a majority of votes with a minimum of two to award a point.
  - o A Red or White Flag will signify one point for that contestant.
  - o A "No See" (crossed flags in front of the corner judge's eyes) is excluded from the vote.
  - o A "No Point" (crossed flags towards the ground) takes away one Red and one White Flag.
  - o A contact warning must be confirmed by two votes.
  - o Two contact warnings, causing bleeding or excessive contact requires immediate disqualification.
  - o A "No Point" decision will be determined in the following scenario:
    - 2 Judges call "Red Point," 1 Judge calls "White Point," 1 Judge calls "No See," 1 Judge calls "No Point"
    - 1 Judge calls "Red Point," 4 Judges call "No See"
  - o If there is a tie at the end of the two-minute match, the competitor that scores the next point will be declared the winner of the match (sudden win rule).

5 Moo Do Values Sparring Competition

Our organization has made considerable strides in laying a foundation that supports an evolution in the way we teach and demonstrate free sparring. The goal is to have our sparring reflect our philosophy represented by the Five Moo Do Values. These values should guide the way we approach all areas of our training. Tournament sparring rules based on the Five Moo Do Values were established and presented for the first time at the 2013 Moment with the Masters. We feel confident if we put the foundation we now have into action; our sparring will evolve into something special and we will continue to evolve as martial artists and human beings.

- Each match is officiated by one referee and four corner judges.
- Each judge will hold a red flag and blue flag to signify each contestant.
- There will be five, 20 second rounds per match. All five rounds will be conducted for each set of competitors.
- The competitor who receives the majority of 5 calls wins the round.
  - o The competitor who wins at least 3 rounds wins the match.
  - o All Five rounds are to be completed even if a competitor has already won 3 rounds.
- Officials will score based on the Five Moo Do Values.

- - o The competitor that demonstrates the best use of both defensive and offensive skills while demonstrating the 5 Moo Do Values in action wins the round.
- Contact warnings will be given to competitors who make contact. 2 contact warnings will result in disqualification.
  - o NOTE: Two contact warnings, causing bleeding or excessive contact requires immediate disqualification.

Regional Team Hyung Competition

Each Region has the opportunity to select multiple teams per division [Effective 2017] to represent them and compete at the National level during the United States Annual National Moo Do Festival each year.

- **Team Selection**
  - o Each Region selects one or more teams (per each division / age category) to represent their Region at the National Festival.
    - The Regional Examiners will review the Team Hyung to ensure the criteria is met.
  - o Each team needs to submit a Video via the Soo Bahk Do Institute for official TAC Review no later than 1 month prior to the National Festival.
    - The TAC will review each Region's Team Hyung to validate that the criteria is met.
    - If the Team Hyung does not meet the expected standard/criteria, the Team will need to make adjustments to the Hyung in order to meet the published criteria or the Team will be disqualified.
- **Team Composition**
  - o All team members must be Dan Members (3 or 4-person team allowed).
  - o **Youth Team** shall be defined as members that are 17 and younger.
  - o **Adult Team** shall be defined as members that are 18 and older.
  - o **Senior Team** shall be defined as members that are 50 and older.
  - o *NOTE:* A Team with 2 adults and 1 youth would be in the Adult Division. A Team with 1 Adult and 2 Youths would be in the Youth Division.
  - o Maximum of two forms can be combined *(example: Passai and Chil Sung Sam Ro Hyung).*
    - Rank appropriate Hyung should be chosen based on the rank of the junior member of the Team.
  - o Maximum of two sparring sequences per Team Form.

- Each sparring sequence will be limited to five techniques per person.
- Either the offensive or defensive technique in any given exchange needs to be taken from one of the two Hyung that have been combined. In other words, if a technique is performed in the sparring sequence that is not from either Hyung, an offensive or defensive technique needs to be performed at the same time to justify the "other" technique's existence in the sparring sequence.
  - No breaking techniques allowed.
  - No acrobatic movements allowed. Tumbling is allowable if justified in a sparring sequence per the requirements listed above.
  - The time limit for Team Hyung is 3 minutes.
  - Any team not meeting the above criteria at the National Competition will be disqualified.
- **Scoring**
  - The Technical Advisory Committee system for scoring Regional Team Hyung consists of 5 judges seated in a straight line facing the team and awarding scores for the Team's performance in the following two areas:
    - Technical Score
    - Artistic Score
  - Forms will be judged according to normal Hyung criteria, group synchronization and creative application.
  - The average of all scores are calculated with the high and low score being disregarded and the remaining three scores averaged to arrive at the Hyung Team's score. The high and low score will be added back in to the average in the event of a tie.
  - *Note:* The TAC or their representatives will meet with the Team Captains prior to the competition and hold a drawing to determine the order of performance.

National Festival info:
https://festival.soobahkdo.org/

Regional Team Sparring Competition

All Regions have the opportunity to select multiple teams per division [Effective 2017] to represent them and compete at the National level during the United States Annual National Moo Do Festival each year.

- **Team Selection**
  - Each Region selects one or more Teams (per each division / age category) to represent their Region at the National Festival.
- **Team Composition**
  - Each team will consist of 5 total participants *(Variable ratio of Male and Female per team)* [Effective 2019].
  - All members must meet the age requirements per the following division categories:
    - Youth Team: 10-12
      - Will consist of 5 participants *(No requirement for number of male or female members)*.
    - Teen Team: 13-17
      - Will consist of 5 participants *(No requirement for number of male or female members)*.
    - Adult Team: 18+
      - Will consist of 5 total participants *(4 Male and 1 Female)*.
- **Rules**
  - The Regional Team Sparring competition will use the same rules as Traditional Point Sparring.
  - The designated TAC Official will meet with the Team Captains before the competition and hold a drawing to determine the Team match brackets.
  - The two teams will line up on the sides of the ring.
  - The center referee will ask both teams to send out their first representative and then alternate thereafter.
    - Note: The two female competitors must compete against each other.
  - The first team to win three matches will be declared the winner.
  - If a tie exists at the end of five matches:
    - The first procedure will be to add all scores (points) together. The team with the higher total of points scored will be declared the winner.
    - The second procedure will be for both Team Captains to select a tie-breaking match between the competitors of their choice (sudden win rule applies).
  - Only the Team Captain is allowed to approach the Center Referee regarding any discrepancies / questions during the match.
    - If discrepancies cannot be resolved, they will be presented to a TAC Official for further review.

Made in the USA
Middletown, DE
25 May 2024

54589817R00073